MATTHEW C. SHAW

Legacy of Wisdom

Timeless life lessons from a father rooted in faith, purpose, & perseverance

Dreamer Reign MEDIA

LEGACY OF WISDOM:
Timeless Life Lessons From a Father Rooted in Faith, Purpose, & Perseverance

Copyright 2024 by Matthew C. Shaw

All rights reserved. No part of this publication may be reproduced, distributed or transmitted in any form or by any means, without prior written permission. Unless otherwise identified, scripture quotations are from the New Living and King James versions of the Bible. New Living Translation, Copyright 1996, 2004, 2015 by Tyndale House Foundation.

Dreamer Reign Media
P.O. BOX 291354
Port Orange, Florida 32129

www.dreamerreign.com

For Worldwide Distribution
Printed in the U.S.A.
ISBN: 978-1-952253-38-6

ENDORSEMENTS

"I do believe you're on to something! I think this will truly be powerful; I love it. I can see this being a legit hit! I can't wait..."
—*Sevarrest Allen, Orlando Magic Sous Chef*

"I really like the layout of your book. It is very motivational yet contains substance...I'm impressed!"
—*Pastor Jamie Jones, Senior Pastor Trinity Church, Deltona, Florida*

"Looks like a beautiful message to our future generations and I can relate to it. I didn't have a father around for most of my life, only my mother and my heavenly father. This book will offer guidance and direction to many people that grew up with similar circumstances."
—*David Morales, Entrepreneur*

"The teaser left me wanting more! I can't wait until the book comes out!"
—*Mike Pedraza, Federal Postal Operations Specialist*

"Makes me want to learn more!"
—*Felice Mathieu, Chaplain & Marriage and Family Therapy Counselor*

"I read that teaser and it was really good."
—*Edwin Carrasquillo, Aerospace Maintenance Engineer*

"Love the concept...Personally love the quote, 'people over profit!' That's FIRE! Also the chapter on inner strength sounds great as it can help people realize they are not alone in their battles. I pray blessings over you and the people who read the book."
—*Pastor Will Manzano, Executive Pastor Trinity Church, Deltona, Florida*

"I like the 'Finding and Living with Purpose' and 'Resilience and Growth through Trials' sections. 'Using Money with Integrity" is a section that is grounded in ethics..."
—*Adrian Drummond CEO and Founder, Braincloud*

"It's incredible how this book reflects the lessons you've mastered and the wisdom you've drawn from others around you. It's a testament to living a Godly life, prioritizing constant growth, and keeping God first, followed by family, business, and friendship."
— *Elliot Rodriguez, Executive*

CONTENTS

Endorsements 3

Dedication 7

Acknowledgements 9

Foreword 10

Introduction 11

Grand Rising Day 1: 13
You Have Seeds Of Greatness! Water Them!

Grand Rising Day 2: 17
Trust In The Lord

Grand Rising Day 3: 21
Ask God For Wisdom

Grand Rising Day 4: 25
Live with Integrity - Speak The Truth - Live Above Reproach!

Grand Rising Day 5: 31
Embrace Cleanliness and Compassion:
"Lessons from a Clean Garbage Can"

Grand Rising Day 6: 35
Look Good! Feel Good!

Grand Rising Day 7: 39
Pay Attention!

Grand Rising Day 8: 45
The devil finds work for idle hands; Stay Purposeful and Productive!

Grand Rising Day 9: 49
Choose your friends and your associations wisely

Grand Rising Day 10: 53
Choose your Hard

Grand Rising Day 11: 59
Be careful not to harbor hate or animosity in your heart.

Grand Rising Day 12: 63
Do NOT worry, God's got you!

Grand Rising Day 13: 67
Be open to criticism from those you trust

Grand Rising Day 14: 71
Control Your Words

Grand Rising Day 15: 75
Be inspired to keep hope alive, even in challenging times

Grand Rising Day 16: 79
Don't Follow Your Heart or your Flesh... Follow God's Wisdom

Grand Rising Day 17: 83
Using money with integrity

Grand Rising Day 18: 89
Always have a Positive Mental attitude!

Grand Rising Day 19: 93
Develop a heart of Gratitude: "Have an Attitude of Gratitude"

Grand Rising Day 20: 97
Find a mentor: "You are limited to the knowledge in your own mind."

Grand Rising Day 21: 105
You have Potential! Turn it into something great!

Grand Rising Day 22: 109
What to do when things aren't going your way.

Grand Rising Day 23: 115
Embrace Your Inner Warrior: Drawing Strength from God, the Ultimate Warrior

Grand Rising Day 24: 121
Read many books but live in the Bible

Grand Rising Day 25 127
One of the most important decisions you can make.

Grand Rising Day 26: 133
Guard and Control your mind: Put a bouncer at the door of your mind!

Grand Rising Day 27: 137
Guard your health and your purity: Your body is a temple of God

Grand Rising Day 28: 143
Money Tips!

Grand Rising Day 29: 149
Self-development: "Make Personal Growth a daily priority"

Grand Rising Day 30: 155
Look to be helpful and generous.

Grand Rising Day 31: 159
Finish what you started! Finish Strong.

Grand Rising Day 32: 165
Now it's your turn!

Endnotes.. 172

DEDICATION

I dedicate this book to you, the reader. I'm writing this as a father—for those who didn't or don't have a father or may need a father figure in their lives. As a father, I want to tell you that I love you—unconditionally. I'm proud of you. Proud that you picked up this book, proud of your willingness to learn and grow into a better person. You are worth it, so keep moving forward toward your goals, dreams, and the amazing life you hope for! You can do it.

If you've recently fallen on hard times or feel like you're worth very little, know this: you are worth more than diamonds or gold. I'm rooting for you! You have what it takes to get up and fight one more time. I'm on the sidelines, cheering for you. YOU have what it takes!

With love,
Dad

To Alex and Ivy Shaw, who transitioned into eternity in 2015, so much of who I am today stems from the values and lessons you instilled in me. Thank you for nurturing my confidence and love for the Lord from an early age. Though you are no longer here physically, your presence lives within me daily through the memories and wisdom you've left behind. I trust you are proud of the man I've become. You are both my angels.

To my mentors, Toby and Mia Ayers, thank you for believing in me and pushing me to grow without coddling. I'm forever grateful.

To my son Maximus, I want you to experience all the things I have—and even those I haven't. I am incredibly proud of the young man you've become and excited to see you grow into both a gentleman and a warrior for Christ.

To my lovely wife, Ashley, thank you for reading, re-reading, and editing my manuscripts, for always believing in me, and for never doubting what we can accomplish together. I love you. I love you. I love you. I would marry you again and again. God got it right when He made you just for me. I couldn't imagine doing life with anyone else. Thank you, and I love you.

To my Goddaughter Nora, I love you and look forward to watching you grow into a strong, confident and beautiful woman.

To my son Leonidas, You are already a blessing, even in the womb. Your mother and I are eagerly anticipating the moment we hold you in our arms and speak life into you. God has extraordinary plans for your life, and we are excited to witness how you will walk in His purpose and make this world a brighter, better place.

My future son/my daughter, I wrote this book with you in mind, thinking about the trials and temptations you may face. I wanted to give you a gift—a gift from my heart to yours. These are the truths your mother and I live by daily, and they have brought us great success spiritually, relationally, and financially. Your mother and I believe these principles will help you stand on our shoulders and achieve even greater success, impacting the world in ways we can only imagine.

Godspeed—we love you.

This book isn't a comprehensive guide, but rather to help you make the right decisions.

Stay strong in the Lord,
Mom & Dad

ACKNOWLEDGEMENTS

- Pastor Jamie: Thank you for preaching with Holy Ghost fire every week and fearlessly addressing the controversial topics that need to be spoken. "Rightly dividing the word of Truth!"
- To my mother-in-law, Mrs. Roz: Thank you for loving me unconditionally. I love and appreciate you. Thank you for giving me the most amazing blessing in the world—your daughter!
- To Pops (Major): Thank you for taking me to that family reunion/book release (or whatever that event was). It inspired me to complete this book. Cheers to you!
- To my sister Faith: Thanks for naming me.
- Dr. John C. Maxwell: For the simple yet profound advice—how to start writing is to just start writing.
- Bishop Dale C. Bronner: Your faith-filled words have always encouraged and strengthened me. You are one of my heroes.
- Larry Winters: You are my mentor's mentor, and you've mentored me from afar. Thank you for your wisdom.
- Gary Ayers: For always standing for righteousness and doing what's right, no matter the circumstances.
- Pastor Joel Hunter: For offering guidance to a young, inexperienced man during your time at Northland Church.
- Pastor Gus Davies: For marrying my wife and me, and for your humble words of wisdom.
- Ainsworth Shaw: My big brother, thank you for encouraging me to marry my wife.
- Avery Shaw: My other big brother, thank you for always being joyful and encouraging.
- Karen Shaw: My older sister, thank you for the interesting conversations.
- Pastor Josh McCain: Thank you for reminding me to write this book no matter the circumstances. You said it would be a powerful tool for fathers and could change lives for generations.
- Felice Mathie: My lifelong friend, thank you for filling me with wisdom, even though we don't talk or hang out as much as we should.

FOREWORD

I have written this book is because to make a difference in the world—to leave an imprint that says, "The world is a better place because I was here." I want to do my part, and I hope you feel the same way.

"For God so loved the world that He gave His only Son." Thankfully, we aren't asked to give our sons or daughters, but maybe we can give in other ways—our time, encouragement, positivity, or support to a cause. Even something as simple as a smile can brighten someone's day. I hope the words in this book touch you and inspire you to leave your own imprint on this world.

"If you are going to achieve excellence in big things, you develop the habit in little things. Excellence is not an exception, it is a prevailing attitude."
- Colin Powell

"Adversity causes some men to break and others to break records!"
- William Arthur Ward

INTRODUCTION

This book has been deeply important for me to write for my children, and I hope it blesses you as well. According to Pew Research Center and Census.gov, the percentage of children living with both parents has dropped since 1968, while the number growing up with only their mother has doubled.[1] For decades, the share of U.S. children in single-parent homes has continued to rise, alongside a decrease in marriage rates and an increase in births outside of marriage. In fact, a recent Pew Research Center study of 130 countries and territories shows that the U.S. has the world's highest rate of children living in single-parent households, with almost a quarter of American children growing up in single-parent homes—this figure is higher than any other country.[2][3]

Growing up without a father can significantly affect a child's development, often leading to higher rates of poverty, lower academic performance, and an increased risk of behavioral and emotional challenges. These realities emphasize the crucial role father figures play in providing structure, security, and positive role models for children. While single mothers are capable of raising good men, a father figure provides something unique that complements a mother's influence, just as mothers offer qualities that fathers cannot replicate.

If you grew up in a single-parent household or faced challenges in your relationship with your father or father figure, I hope this book helps bridge that gap by offering encouragement and guidance. My desire is to leave a meaningful imprint on this world and make it better because I was here—and I hope this book inspires you to do the same.

Legacy of Wisdom is designed to provide daily guidance in an accessible and meaningful way. At the start of each chapter, you'll find the greeting **"GRAND RISING."** More than just a way to say "good morning," it embodies the idea of beginning each day with purpose, positivity, and intentionality. It serves as a reminder of the power in how we start our days, the words we speak, and the actions we choose. Each chapter, labeled as Grand Rising Day 1, Grand Rising Day 2, and so on, is crafted for quick, daily reading, making it easy to incorporate into even the busiest of schedules. The structure of each chapter begins with a title that sets the tone for the day's lesson, followed by a personal excerpt drawn from my experiences, studies, or reflections. This is supported by secular quotes that offer additional perspectives and wisdom, and then tied together with relevant Bible verses to ground the teachings in Scripture. Finally, each chapter concludes with affirmations—positive declarations that encourage readers to internalize and apply the lesson. Through this structure, Legacy of Wisdom provides a balanced blend of inspiration, reflection, and motivation to empower readers to rise each day with intention and focus.

"For God so loved the world that He gave His only Son." Thankfully, we're not asked to give up our sons or daughters, but we can give in other ways: through our time, encouragement, positivity, or support for a cause. Even something as simple as a smile can brighten someone's day. I hope the words in this book inspire you to leave your own positive mark on the world.

GRAND RISING
DAY ONE

YOU HAVE SEEDS OF GREATNESS! WATER THEM!

You have seeds of greatness inside of you! God has amazing plans for you. You were built and formed in the womb for greatness! Accept the fact that you were destined for something great!

"Your mother and I prayed over you before you were ever conceived. While you were in the womb we prayed over your health, mental capacities, spiritual fortitude and your spouse later on in life. The Lord has big plans for your life. No matter what anyone else wants you to do, you must follow your calling to serve the Lord."

These are the things that I have prayed over my children. Even if your parents haven't prayed these positive confessions over your life or been the best example, let's start fresh. These positive confessions are yours now. I am praying over your life, your physical and mental health, and your overall well-being. It doesn't matter what you have gone through or what your current or future circumstances look like.

The seeds of greatness that are planted inside of you remind me of the story of the bamboo tree. When a bamboo seed is planted, it requires a lot of care. The seed must be watered and fertilized consistently. In the first year, there are no visible signs of growth. This continues into the second year, the third year, the fourth year, and even into the fifth year. Despite the lack of visible progress, the farmer must continue to nurture the seed with the same dedication and care.

Then, suddenly, in the fifth year, the bamboo tree begins to grow at an astonishing rate. Within just six weeks, it can grow as much as 90 feet tall. The reason for this sudden growth is that during the first five years, the bamboo was developing a strong, extensive root system underground, which was necessary to support its future rapid growth.

This story is often used to illustrate the importance of persistence and patience. I want to remind you that just because you don't see immediate results doesn't mean that nothing is happening. You must continue to lay the groundwork, (plant and water the seeds) that are crucial for future success and growth.

You are special, absolutely loved, and built for greatness! Dream big and expect amazing things from your life. You are a champion!

Quotes:

"Every champion was once a contender who refused to give up."

– Rocky Balboa

"You were born to win, but to be a winner, you must plan to win, prepare to win, and expect to win."

– Zig Ziglar

"A champion is someone who gets up when he can't."

– Jack Dempsey

"To be a great champion you must believe you are the best. If you're not, pretend you are."

– Unknown

"Champions aren't made in gyms...Champions are made from something they have deep inside them-a desire, a dream, a vision. They have to have the skill, and the will. But the will must be stronger than the skill."

– Muhammad Ali

"Champions aren't made in the ring, they are merely recognized there..."

– Joe Frazier

"I like the dreams of the future better than the history of the past."

– Thomas Jefferson

Bible Verses:

"For I know the plans I have for you," declares the Lord, "plans to prosper you and not to harm you, plans to give you hope and a future."
-Jeremiah 29:11 (NIV)

"Before I formed you in the womb I knew you, before you were born I set you apart; I appointed you as a prophet to the nations."
-Jeremiah 1:5 (KJV)

"For many are called, but few are chosen."
-Matthew 22:14 (NKJV)

"All praise to God, the Father of our Lord Jesus Christ, who has blessed us with every spiritual blessing in the heavenly realms because we are united with Christ. Even before he made the world, God loved us and chose us in Christ to be holy and without fault in his eyes."
-Ephesians 1:3-4 (NLT)

"I pray that your hearts will be flooded with light so that you can understand the confident hope he has given to those he called—his holy people who are his rich and glorious inheritance. I also pray that you will understand the incredible greatness of God's power for us who believe him. This is the same mighty power that raised Christ from the dead and seated him in the place of honor at God's right hand in the heavenly realms."
-Ephesians 1:18-20 (NLT)

Today's Affirmations:

- I have seeds of greatness planted within me!
- God has incredible plans for my life!
- I am destined for something great and I embrace my calling.
- My roots are growing strong, even when I don't see immediate results.
- I am patient and persistent, knowing that my breakthrough is coming.
- I am special, loved, and built for greatness!
- I am more than a conqueror through Christ.
- I rise up with the heart of a champion.
- I trust God's timing and His plans to prosper me.
- I walk confidently in the power of God's love and purpose for my life.

with love,
Dad

GRAND RISING DAY TWO

TRUST IN THE LORD

Follow God's principles, not man's. Do not depend on your own understanding or the wisdom of this world. Early in my business career, I partnered with some people I went to college with, believing they were trustworthy. Years later, I discovered they were not. They betrayed us, stealing business and plotting against my family. It was shocking when they even grew upset after we paid off my wife's student loans and began improving our financial situation. I was so confused—shouldn't they have been happy for us? But they weren't. They had taken advantage of our financial vulnerability to maintain leverage over us.
(In hindsight, I realize I was naive and missed the warning signs. This experience matured me significantly.)

At that time in our lives, we heavily relied on people and what we believed they could do. But after that experience, we started to place our trust fully in the Lord to guide us through challenging situations. One notable example was our decision to tithe consistently, even when we didn't think we could afford it. In Malachi 3:10, the Lord invites us to test Him in this area, promising that the floodgates of blessings will open. Time and time again, we received unexpected checks in the mail and extra money in our bank account when we needed it most.

Trusting the Lord isn't always easy, especially when past experiences with broken promises have made it difficult. But one thing is certain—our Father in heaven never breaks His promises. What He says WILL ALWAYS come to pass.

Quotes:

"Put your shoulder to the wheel and God will bless the rest."

— Ivy Shaw (My mother)

"The simple secret is this: put your trust in the Lord, do your best, then leave the rest to Him."

— Joseph B. Wirthlin

"Trust in the Lord is the only true antidote to fear. Focusing on God rather than the trial will keep us from sinking in fear. However, learning to face our fears does not mean we will never have another anxious moment. Faith does not lie in trusting God to stop the storm, but in trusting Him to enable us to walk through the storm. When trouble occurs, He will give us the ability to cope with it."

— Jill Briscoe

"Trials may come - and we may not understand everything that happens to us or around us. But if we humbly, quietly trust in the Lord, He will give us guidance and strength in every challenge we face. When our only desire is to please Him, we will be blessed with a deep inner peace."

— Bruce D. Porter

"If we will put our trust in the Lord, He will help us through our difficulties, whatever they may be."

— Thomas S. Monson

"The saddest thing about betrayal is that it never comes from your enemies."

— Anonymous

"The only true wisdom is in knowing you know nothing."

— Socrates

"We cannot solve our problems with the same thinking we used when we created them."

— Albert Einstein

"Faith is taking the first step even when you don't see the whole staircase."

— Martin Luther King Jr.

Bible Verses:

"Since you have been raised to new life with Christ, set your sights on the realities of heaven, where Christ sits in the place of honor at God's right hand. Think about the things of heaven, not the things of earth. For you died to this life, and your real life is hidden with Christ in God. And when Christ, who is your life, is revealed to the whole world, you will share in all his glory."

-Colossians 3:1-4 (NLT)

"But those who trust in the Lord will find new strength. They will soar high on wings like eagles. They will run and not grow weary. They will walk and not faint."

-Isaiah 40:31 (NLT)

"So be strong and courageous! Do not be afraid and do not panic before them. For the Lord your God will personally go ahead of you. He will neither fail you nor abandon you."

-Deuteronomy 31:6 (KJV)

"And we know that God causes everything to work together for the good of those who love God and are called according to his purpose for them."

-Romans 8:28 (NLT)

"Trust in the Lord with all your heart; do not depend on your own understanding. Seek his will in all you do, and he will show you which path to take."

-Proverbs 3:5-6 (NLT)

"But blessed are those who trust in the Lord and have made the Lord their hope and confidence."

-Jeremiah 17:7 (NLT)

"It is not an enemy who taunts me—I could bear that. It is not my foes who so arrogantly insult me—I could have hidden from them. Instead, it is you—my equal, my companion and close friend. What good fellowship we once enjoyed as we walked together to the house of God."

-Psalm 55:12-14 (NLT)

"God is not a man, so he does not lie. He is not human, so he does not change his mind. Has he ever spoken and failed to act? Has he ever promised and not carried it through?"

-Numbers 23:19 (NLT)

"It is the same with my word. I send it out, and it always produces fruit. It will accomplish all I want it to, and it will prosper everywhere I send it."

-Isaiah 55:11 (NLT)

"Give, and you will receive. Your gift will return to you in full—pressed down, shaken together to make room for more, running over, and poured into your lap. The amount you

give will determine the amount you get back."
-Luke 6:38 (NLT)

"And this same God who takes care of me will supply all your needs from his glorious riches, which have been given to us in Christ Jesus."
-Philippians 4:19 (NLT)

"We can rejoice, too, when we run into problems and trials, for we know that they help us develop endurance. And endurance develops strength of character, and character strengthens our confident hope of salvation."
-Romans 5:3-4 (NLT)

Today's Affirmations:

- I trust in the Lord with all my heart and lean not on my own understanding.
- I follow God's principles, not man's, knowing He will guide my steps.
- God is my provider; I trust Him to meet all my needs in every situation.
- No weapon formed against me shall prosper because God is with me.
- I release control and allow the Lord to guide me through storms and trials.
- God's promises never fail; He will open the floodgates of blessings in my life.
- I have strength, courage, and peace because I trust in the Lord's plan.
- All things work together for my good because I love and serve God.
- My trust in the Lord brings health and nourishment to my body and soul.
- I seek first the Kingdom of God, and everything I need is added to me.

GRAND RISING DAY THREE

Ask God For Wisdom

You have probably heard the saying, "Knowledge is power." However, having knowledge is not enough; it's about applying what you know. Knowledge becomes power when it is transformed into wisdom through action!

For years, I knew that working out and eating healthy were the right choices, yet I lived a sedentary lifestyle and indulged in unhealthy eating habits, which led to weight gain. As I write this book, I am actively applying my knowledge of healthy living. This commitment has made me healthier, lowered my blood pressure, reduced my stress, and sharpened my focus. These improvements enable me to write with clarity and purpose.

Solomon, renowned in the Bible as the wisest man who ever lived, simply asked God for wisdom. God was so pleased with Solomon's request for wisdom instead of wealth or fame that He blessed him with those extra gifts as well. Solomon sought to be a good steward of what God had already given him (1 Kings 3:6-14).

When facing decisions, whether it's buying a house, a car, making an investment, starting a business or who to marry, ask God for wisdom. Seek

His guidance and discernment. As James 4:2 (KJV) reminds us, "Ye have not, because ye ask not."

There is much importance in seeking wisdom through experience and understanding rather than merely accumulating information. The Book of Proverbs is filled with wisdom. With 31 chapters, you can read one chapter each day of the month. Since today is Day 3, read Proverbs chapter 3, which focuses on trusting in the Lord. This daily practice will deposit wisdom into your heart, soul, and mind.

Quotes:

"Knowledge speaks, but wisdom listens."

- Jimi Hendrix

"Wisdom is the reward you get for a lifetime of listening when you'd have preferred to talk."

- Mark Twain

"An ounce of action is worth a ton of theory."

- Ralph Waldo Emerson

"The greatest danger in times of turbulence is not the turbulence—it is to act with yesterday's logic."

- Peter Drucker

"In the middle of difficulty lies opportunity."

- Albert Einstein

"A wise man will make more opportunities than he finds."

- Francis Bacon

"The only real mistake is the one from which we learn nothing."

- Henry Ford

"The unexamined life is not worth living."

- Socrates

"Your worldly obligations can cloud your spiritual judgment."

-Pastor Jamie Jones

Bible Verses:

"For the wisdom of this world is foolishness to God. As the Scriptures say, 'He traps the wise in the snare of their own cleverness.'"
-1 Corinthians 3:19 (NLT)

"This foolish plan of God is wiser than the wisest of human plans, and God's weakness is stronger than the greatest of human strength."
-1 Corinthians 1:25 (NLT)

"Joyful is the person who finds wisdom, the one who gains understanding."
-Proverbs 3:13 (NLT)

"For the Lord grants wisdom! From his mouth come knowledge and understanding."
-Proverbs 2:6 (NLT)

"Getting wisdom is the wisest thing you can do! And whatever else you do, develop good judgment. If you prize wisdom, she will make you great. Embrace her, and she will honor you. She will place a lovely wreath on your head; she will present you with a beautiful crown."
-Proverbs 4:7-9 (NLT)

"If you need wisdom, ask our generous God, and he will give it to you. He will not rebuke you for asking."
-James 1:5 (NLT)

"But don't just listen to God's word. You must do what it says. Otherwise, you are only fooling yourselves."
-James 1:22 (NLT)

"Work willingly at whatever you do, as though you were working for the Lord rather than for people."
-Colossians 3:23 (NLT)

"Trust in the Lord with all your heart; do not depend on your own understanding. Seek his will in all you do, and he will show you which path to take."
-Proverbs 3:5-6 (NLT)

"Plans go wrong for lack of advice; many advisers bring success."
-Proverbs 15:22 (NLT)

"Let the wise listen to these proverbs and become even wiser. Let those who understand receive guidance."
-Proverbs 1:5 (NLT)

"Don't copy the behavior and customs of this world, but let God transform you into a new person by changing the way you think. Then you will learn to know God's will for you, which

LEGACY OF WISDOM

is good and pleasing and perfect."
-Romans 12:2 (NLT)
"Instead, let us test and examine our ways. Let us turn back to the Lord."
-Lamentations 3:40 (NLT)

Today's Affirmations:

- I seek and apply wisdom daily in every aspect of my life.
- God generously grants me wisdom when I ask in faith.
- I am a good steward of the blessings and knowledge I've received.
- My knowledge becomes power through action and discernment.
- I trust God to guide my decisions in all matters, large and small.
- As I apply wisdom, I experience improved health, clarity, and purpose.
- I honor my body by living a healthy lifestyle and making wise choices.
- I gain strength, focus, and peace through God's wisdom.
- Each day, I grow wiser and more understanding through God's Word.
- God is my source of wisdom, and I embrace it fully without doubt.
- I am single-minded and stable in everything I do

GRAND RISING
DAY FOUR

LIVE WITH INTEGRITY - SPEAK THE TRUTH
LIVE ABOVE REPROACH!

Something that my lovely mother Ivy Shaw always said to me as I was growing up was "Speak the truth and speak it ever, cost it what it will, he who hides the wrong he does, does the wrong thing still…"

So speak the truth whatever the cost may be. When you speak the truth you never have to remember a story or a lie you told. It makes life easier and keeps your integrity high.

I am a history buff so a really famous story that comes to my mind when it comes to dis-integrity is Former President Richard Nixon. President Richard Nixon is most famously associated with the Watergate scandal, a major political scandal in the United States during the early 1970s. The scandal stemmed from a break-in at the Democratic National Committee headquarters at the Watergate office complex in Washington, D.C., and the Nixon administration's attempted cover-up of its involvement.

Nixon and his administration initially denied any involvement. However, investigative journalism, particularly by reporters Bob Woodward and Carl Bernstein of The Washington Post, helped uncover evidence of a broader pattern of abuses of power by the Nixon administration. This included wiretapping, political espionage, and attempts to sabotage political opponents.

A critical moment in the unraveling of the cover-up was the revelation of secret tape recordings made in the Oval Office. These tapes provided clear evidence that Nixon had been involved in efforts to obstruct justice and had lied to the public and investigators about his knowledge of the break-in and subsequent cover-up.

President Richard Nixon famously declared, "I am not a crook," during a press conference on November 17, 1973, at the Associated Press Managing Editors annual conference at Walt Disney World in Orlando, Florida. This statement was in response to growing allegations of financial improprieties and the ongoing investigations related to the Watergate scandal. Nixon insisted that he had not profited from public service and denied any wrongdoing, but the evidence gathered in the subsequent months, particularly the release of the White House tapes, ultimately contradicted his claims and faced with impending impeachment, Nixon resigned on August 8, 1974, becoming the only U.S. president to resign from office. The Watergate scandal significantly eroded public trust in government and remains a pivotal moment in American political history.

A more recent historical example that I lived through and had the opportunity to watch unfold was the Bill Clinton - Monica Lewinsky Scandal. The scandal involved a sexual relationship between President Clinton and the then 22-year-old White House intern Monica Lewinsky from 1995 to 1997. The affair was exposed in 1998 through taped conversations by Lewinsky's confidant, Linda Tripp. Clinton initially denied the allegations in a now-infamous televised address on January 26, 1998, saying, "I did not have sexual relations with that woman, Miss Lewinsky."

Despite Clinton's initial denial, physical evidence, including a blue dress belonging to Lewinsky that was stained with Clinton's semen, emerged. In August 1998, Clinton admitted to having an "inappropriate relationship" with Lewinsky in a grand jury testimony and later addressed the nation, acknowledging his misconduct. This led to his impeachment by the House of Representatives for perjury and obstruction of justice in December 1998. However, the Senate acquitted him in February 1999, and he remained in office. The scandal had lasting effects on the individuals involved and on American politics. Clinton completed his second term in office, but this scandal tarnished his legacy.

Pretty embarrassing stuff right? For me it was the legacy that both of these presidents left. Both of their legacies are absolutely tarnished. Former President Nixon is forever considered a liar a untrustworthy politician, and a crook. Former President Clinton on September 30, 1998, announced that the federal budget, which had been in deficit for 29 years, had been balanced and would run a surplus of approximately $70 billion for the fiscal year. Despite this significant achievement, his legacy is more often associated with his infidelity and dishonesty. Integrity is a choice. So choose to be truthful and live with integrity. Be honest and clear in everything that you do.

Quotes:

"Speak the truth and speak it ever, cost it what it will, he who hides the wrong he does, does the wrong thing still..."
– Ivy Shaw

"There's just some magic in truth and honesty and openness."
– Frank Ocean

"Honesty is more than not lying. It is truth telling, truth speaking, truth living, and truth loving."
– James E. Faust

"Develop your character so that you are a person of integrity."
– Peter Cain

"Moral authority comes from following universal and timeless principles like honesty, integrity, and treating people with respect."
– Stephen Covey

"Supporting the truth, even when it is unpopular, shows the capacity for honesty and integrity."
– Steve Brunkhorst

"There is a price to pay for speaking the truth. There is a bigger price for living a lie."
– Cornel West

"It is better to be divided by truth than to be united in error. It is better to speak the truth that hurts and then heals, than falsehood that comforts and then kills. It is better to be hated for telling the truth than to be loved for telling a lie. It is better to stand alone with the truth, than to be wrong with a multitude. It is better to ultimately succeed with the truth than to temporarily succeed with a lie. There is only one Gospel."
– Adrian Rogers

"Speak the truth. Transparency breeds legitimacy."

– John C. Maxwell

Bible Verses:

"Let there be no sexual immorality, impurity, or greed among you. Such sins have no place among God's people. Obscene stories, foolish talk, and coarse jokes—these are not for you. Instead, let there be thankfulness to God. You can be sure that no immoral, impure, or greedy person will inherit the Kingdom of Christ and of God. For a greedy person is an idolater, worshiping the things of this world. Don't be fooled by those who try to excuse these sins, for the anger of God will fall on all who disobey him. Don't participate in the things these people do. For once you were full of darkness, but now you have light from the Lord. So live as people of light! For this light within you produces only what is good and right and true."

-Ephesians 5:3-9 (NLT)

"An elder must live a blameless life. He must be faithful to his wife, and his children must be believers who don't have a reputation for being wild or rebellious."

-Titus 1:6 (NLT)

"The LORD detests lying lips, but he delights in those who tell the truth."

-Proverbs 12:22 (NLT)

"The godly walk with integrity; blessed are their children who follow them."

-Proverbs 20:7 (NLT)

"Honesty guides good people; dishonesty destroys treacherous people."

-Proverbs 11:3 (NLT)

"For the Scriptures say, 'If you want to enjoy life and see many happy days, keep your tongue from speaking evil and your lips from telling lies.'"

-1 Peter 3:10 (NLT)

"He grants a treasure of common sense to the honest. He is a shield to those who walk with integrity."

-Proverbs 2:7 (NLT)

Today's Affirmations:

- I live with integrity in every aspect of my life.
- I choose honesty and transparency, no matter the cost.
- I speak the truth boldly, trusting that truth brings freedom.
- I honor God by living above reproach in my words and actions.
- I am committed to being truthful, even when it is difficult or unpopular.
- My legacy will be one of integrity, honesty, and righteousness.
- I am guided by timeless principles of truth and respect for others.
- I embrace the light of truth and reject deceit and dishonesty.
- I align my character with God's standards, living blamelessly before Him.
- I live as a person of light, reflecting goodness, righteousness, and truth.

with love,
Dad

GRAND RISING DAY FIVE

Embrace Cleanliness and Compassion
"Lessons from a Clean Garbage Can"

I was around 12 or 13 years old when I saw my father washing out our garbage can. I asked him, "Why are you washing a garbage can? It's supposed to be dirty." My dad looked at me over his glasses and said, "Matthew, just because it's a garbage can doesn't mean it has to be dirty." For some reason, this lesson stuck with me. It seemed to go far beyond the garbage can.

I applied this lesson to my life, learning to keep my surroundings clean—my house, my room, my car, my clothes, my shoes, and myself. If we care enough to keep a garbage can clean, we should certainly care about where we lay our heads to sleep. Don't litter, and always pick up your trash. At the time of writing this book, it is estimated that the Great Pacific Garbage Patch holds around 1.8 trillion pieces of plastic, weighing approximately 80,000 metric tons. Even space is now littered, with debris posing serious risks to active satellites. This global carelessness reflects more than just a disregard for the planet—it highlights a deeper neglect of our role as stewards of God's creation.

Paul, in his letter to the Philippians, gives us a startling perspective on what's truly valuable. He says, "I consider everything a loss because of the surpassing worth of knowing Christ Jesus my Lord, for whose sake I have lost

all things. I consider them garbage, that I may gain Christ" (Philippians 3:8, NIV). Paul wasn't simply speaking about physical possessions but about the mindset of valuing the eternal over the temporary. He saw the pursuits of this world as trash when compared to the priceless value of knowing Christ.
But here's the twist: the world doesn't take this stance. Just as we've neglected the earth through pollution and waste, we've also neglected the care of our souls. People cling to the very things Paul calls "garbage" — wealth, status, fleeting pleasures — while discarding the treasures of faith, integrity, and love for others.

As I grew older, this lesson also shaped how I treat people. Just because society may treat a group of people poorly doesn't mean I should. I often think about how people treat the homeless, stepping over them or judging them for their circumstances. But we don't know their stories, and we are all God's people. We should treat everyone with love, dignity, and respect. This parallels the idea that just because something—or someone—is seen as disposable by society doesn't mean it lacks value in God's eyes.

If you take pride in keeping your garbage can clean, you'll take pride in keeping everything else in your life clean. My mother always said, "Cleanliness is next to godliness!" And she was right—not just in the physical sense but in how we approach our relationships, responsibilities, and spiritual lives. Taking care of what God has given us—be it the earth, our homes, or the people around us—is an act of gratitude and worship.

<u>Quotes</u>:

"Just because it's a garbage can doesn't mean it has to be dirty."

— Junior Shaw

"Don't trash your future. Keep your surroundings clean.'"

— Unknown

"There is a story behind every person. There is a reason why they are the way they are. Think about that, and respect them for who they are.'

— Unknown

"You can easily judge the character of a man by how he treats those who can do nothing for him."

— Malcolm S. Forbes.

"Set an example. Treat everyone with kindness and respect, even those who

are rude to you, not because they are nice, but because you are."
— Roy T. Bennett

"Sanitation and cleanliness are among the humblest of the civic virtues, and it is easy to underestimate the significance."
— Ram Nath Kovind

"Cleanliness is a state of purity, clarity, and precision."
— Suze Orman

"Order is the shape upon which beauty depends."
— Pearl S. Buck

"Be kind, for everyone you meet is fighting a hard battle."
— Attributed to Ian Maclaren (Rev. John Watson)

"The true measure of a man is how he treats someone who can do him absolutely no good."
— Samuel Johnson

"Our prime purpose in this life is to help others. And if you can't help them, at least don't hurt them."
— Dalai Lama

"We do not inherit the earth from our ancestors, we borrow it from our children."
— Native American Proverb

"The environment is where we all meet; where we all have a mutual interest; it is the one thing all of us share."
— Lady Bird Johnson

Bible Verses:

"Since God chose you to be the holy people he loves, you must clothe yourselves with tenderhearted mercy, kindness, humility, gentleness, and patience."
-Colossians 3:12 (NLT)

"The LORD is good to everyone. He showers compassion on all his creation."
-Psalm 145:9 (NLT)

"But be sure that everything is done properly and in order."
-1 Corinthians 14:40 (NLT)

"I walked by the field of a lazy person, the vineyard of one with no common sense. I saw that it was overgrown with nettles. It was covered with weeds, and its walls were broken down."
-Proverbs 24:30-31 (NLT)

"Do to others whatever you would like them to do to you. This is the essence of all that is taught in the law and the prophets."
-Matthew 7:12 (NLT) (Known as the Golden Rule)

"If you help the poor, you are lending to the Lord—and he will repay you!"
-Proverbs 19:17 (NLT)

"My dear brothers and sisters, how can you claim to have faith in our glorious Lord Jesus Christ if you favor some people over others? For example, suppose someone comes into your meeting dressed in fancy clothes and expensive jewelry, and another comes in who is poor and dressed in dirty clothes. If you give special attention and a good seat to the rich person, but you say to the poor one, 'You can stand over there, or else sit on the floor'—well, doesn't this discrimination show that your judgments are guided by evil motives?"
-James 2:1-4 (NLT)

"The Lord God placed the man in the Garden of Eden to tend and watch over it."
-Genesis 2:15 (NLT)

"The earth is the Lord's, and everything in it. The world and all its people belong to him."
-Psalm 24:1 (NLT)

"The godly care for their animals, but the wicked are always cruel."
-Proverbs 12:10 (NLT)

Today's Affirmations:

- I take pride in maintaining cleanliness and order in all aspects of my life.
- I care for the environment by refusing to litter and respecting shared spaces.
- I treat every person with love, dignity, and respect, understanding their inherent worth.
- I lead by example, practicing kindness and respect, even when others don't.
- I honor the spaces I live in, knowing that they reflect my values and character.
- I see cleanliness as a reflection of my commitment to a higher purpose.
- I embrace humility, mercy, and patience in every encounter.
- I appreciate that everyone has a story, and I choose to treat them with grace and compassion.

GRAND RISING DAY SIX

Look Your Best — "Look Good Feel Good!"

For me, "dress to impress" means dressing to impress myself. I take pride in having a nice haircut and looking presentable. Remember, you are essentially a billboard for your personal brand. While we often hear, "don't judge a book by its cover," the reality is that everyone does just that. First impressions, particularly regarding appearance, are crucial. My mother always emphasized, "You must look presentable."

First impressions significantly impact how people perceive you. I'm not suggesting you dress nicely solely to impress others, but conveying a positive and confident image is important—especially when you might be conducting business or aiming to positively influence someone's life. Presenting yourself as confident and well put together can help you land a deal or ensure that others listen to what you have to say.

Dress stylishly at every age, within your budget. When you look good, you feel good and inspired. However, it's essential to balance your pursuit of physical attractiveness with nurturing your inner beauty. While looking good on the outside can boost your confidence, cultivating qualities like kindness, empathy, and integrity is equally important. True beauty comes from within; developing a strong character and a compassionate heart will make you more appealing and respected by others. Remember, external appearances may fade over time, but the beauty of a good heart and noble spirit endures. So, while you invest time in your appearance, also invest in personal growth, building meaningful relationships, and making a positive impact on those around you.

Steve Harvey, a well-dressed comedian, advises that every man should own a black suit, a navy suit, a gray suit, a brown suit, and a tan suit, along with white, powder blue, or cream shirts. With these pieces, you can create 75 different combinations!

Looking good isn't about vanity; it's about having a healthy appreciation for yourself. You take care of what you care about, and since you care about yourself, stay well-groomed and well-dressed. Remember, your body is a temple. While outward appearance matters to people, God values the inner qualities of the heart.

Quotes:

"Dressing is a way of life."

- Yves Saint Laurent

"Fashion is about dressing according to what's fashionable. Style is more about being yourself."

- Oscar de la Renta

"You can never be overdressed or overeducated."

- Oscar Wild

"Dress how you want to be addressed."

- Unknown

"Style is a way to say who you are without having to speak."

- Rachel Zoe

"Beauty begins the moment you decide to be yourself."

- Coco Chanel

"Looking good isn't self-importance; it's self-respect."

- Charles Hix

"Your outer appearance is a reflection of your inner self."

- Unknown

"Life is too short to wear boring clothes."

- Unknown

"What you wear is how you present yourself to the world, especially today, when human contacts are so quick. Fashion is instant language."

- Miuccia Prada

"Confidence is the best outfit. Rock it and own it."

– Unknown

Bible Verses:

"Do you not know that your bodies are temples of the Holy Spirit, who is in you, whom you have received from God? You are not your own; you were bought at a price. Therefore honor God with your bodies."

-1 Corinthians 6:19-20 (NIV)

"Don't be concerned about the outward beauty of fancy hairstyles, expensive jewelry, or beautiful clothes. You should clothe yourselves instead with the beauty that comes from within, the unfading beauty of a gentle and quiet spirit, which is so precious to God."

1 Peter 3:3-4 (NLT)

"You are altogether beautiful, my darling, beautiful in every way."

-Songs of Solomon 4:7 (NLT)

"Wear fine clothes, with a splash of cologne!"

-Ecclesiastes 9:8 (NLT)

"But the Lord said to Samuel, 'Don't judge by his appearance or height, for I have rejected him. The Lord doesn't see things the way you see them. People judge by outward appearance, but the Lord looks at the heart.'"

-1 Samuel 16:7 (NLT)

"Charm is deceptive, and beauty does not last; but a woman who fears the Lord will be greatly praised."

-Proverbs 31:30 (NLT)

"In the same way, let your good deeds shine out for all to see, so that everyone will praise your heavenly Father."

-Matthew 5:16 (NLT)

"Since God chose you to be the holy people he loves, you must clothe yourselves with tenderhearted mercy, kindness, humility, gentleness, and patience. Make allowance for each other's faults, and forgive anyone who offends you. Remember, the Lord forgave you, so you must forgive others. Above all, clothe yourselves with love, which binds us all together in perfect harmony."

-Colossians 3:12-14 (NLT)

"Don't copy the behavior and customs of this world, but let God transform you into a new person by changing the way you think. Then you will learn to know God's will for you, which is good and pleasing and perfect."

-Romans 12:2 (NLT)

Today's Affirmations:

- I dress to impress myself, reflecting my personal brand with confidence.
- I take pride in my appearance, presenting myself with care and attention to detail.
- I honor my body as a temple and invest in my well-being through self-care.
- I nurture my inner beauty by cultivating kindness, empathy, and integrity.
- I exude confidence and inspire others through my positive presence and character.
- I commit to both my physical appearance and personal growth, recognizing their interconnectedness.
- I feel empowered and energized when I look good, embracing each day with confidence.
- My true beauty radiates from within, and I share positivity and strength with those around me.
- I appreciate myself and express this through how I present myself to the world.

with love,
Dad

GRAND RISING DAY SEVEN

PAY ATTENTION!

Have you ever considered how much we miss because we're too distracted to notice the details? Life often speaks to us in whispers—through subtle signs, quiet lessons, and fleeting moments of insight. Paying attention isn't just about seeing what's in front of you; it's about being present, intentional, and aware of what surrounds you, building deeper connections along the way.

Listen Actively:

Engaging communication starts with genuine listening and observation. This goes beyond simply hearing words—it means immersing yourself in the conversation by tuning into the speaker's tone, body language, and emotional cues. By prioritizing listening over speaking, we create space for meaningful dialogue and deeper understanding.

Active listening allows us to absorb the speaker's message while uncovering insights that can shape our own decisions and beliefs. Observing reactions also teaches us what to avoid in similar situations, offering valuable lessons from both positive and negative experiences.

By listening first, we validate others and foster mutual respect, encouraging open and honest exchanges. Patience and thoughtful responses further enhance relationships, deepen understanding, and promote personal growth, making active listening a cornerstone of meaningful connection.

Read Between the Lines:

Effective communication goes beyond words—it requires understanding both what is spoken and what remains unsaid. By observing body language, tone, and facial expressions, we gain insight into others' true emotions and intentions, creating deeper connections and understanding.

My mother often reminded me, "You have two ears and one mouth, two eyes and one mouth. Listen and observe twice as much as you speak." This wisdom emphasizes the value of attentiveness. When we listen and observe carefully, we can respond thoughtfully, tailoring our words to foster empathy and trust.

Unspoken cues often reveal what someone may hesitate to express aloud. By recognizing these subtleties, we create safe spaces for open dialogue, encouraging richer conversations and stronger relationships. This patience and attentiveness also cultivate humility, allowing us to value others' perspectives and experiences.

In every interaction, listening and adapting based on what we hear helps us navigate with greater empathy and awareness. By heeding both spoken and unspoken messages, we not only build meaningful connections but also grow in understanding and respect.

Be Mindful of Distractions:

In today's digital age, smartphones and other devices often pull us away from the present moment. While they offer connection and convenience, they can also become barriers, distracting us from the richness of life happening around us.

A powerful illustration of this phenomenon is a popular image showing an elderly lady standing serenely amidst a bustling crowd. While she is fully engaged with her surroundings, everyone else is glued to their screens, oblivious to the beauty and life unfolding around them. This stark contrast highlights how easily technology can become a barrier to the present moment when it takes precedence over presence.

Mindfulness involves consciously setting aside devices to fully immerse ourselves in our environment. It's about noticing the laughter of children, the warmth of the sun, or the aroma of freshly brewed coffee. These small moments cultivate gratitude and enrich our lives.

Being present also strengthens relationships. By engaging in conversations without distractions, we show respect and build deeper connections. Let's choose to embrace the moment, appreciating the beauty and connections that surround us, and fostering a more engaged and connected life.

Stay Aware of Your Surroundings:

When entering a new place, take a moment to observe your surroundings. Identify exits and watch for anything unusual or out of place. This awareness can be crucial for your safety.

Remember, the devil is here to steal, kill, and destroy, and not everyone you encounter has your best interests at heart. I recall a conversation with my barber, who shared a valuable lesson with his son: trust your instincts and practice discernment. While many may appear friendly or trustworthy, some may have harmful intentions.

By staying vigilant and aware of your environment and the people around you, you can better protect yourself and navigate the world with confidence and security.

Appreciate the Beauty Around You:

In our fast-paced lives, it's easy to overlook the beauty around us. Taking time to notice nature's details can lift our spirits and enrich our lives. Step outside and observe the trees swaying in the breeze, the rustling leaves, and the fresh air filled with earthy scents and blooming flowers.

Notice the shimmering water of nearby lakes, rivers, or oceans, and listen to the soothing sounds of flowing water or crashing waves. Appreciate the animals, from small insects to soaring birds, each contributing to the world's diversity.

Make time to walk in a park or nature trail. Disconnect from the noise of daily life and immerse yourself in the tranquility. Breathe deeply, feel the warmth of the sun, listen to birds, and admire the beauty of leaves and flowers.

By practicing mindfulness and appreciating the wonders around us, we reconnect with life's simple joys and find peace in the beauty always waiting to be noticed. This moment of reflection reminds us to slow down, observe, and embrace the world with open hearts and attentive minds.

Quotes:

"Not everyone is your friend..."

— Jeff Young (Barber)

"When someone shows you who they are, believe them the first time. They know themselves much better than you do."

— Maya Angelou

"It is better to keep your mouth closed and let people think you are a fool than to open it and remove all doubt."

— Mark Twain

"God gave you one mouth, two ears and two eyes...... Listen and observe more than you run your mouth..."

— Ivy Shaw (My mother)

"Loose lips sink ships."

— American English idiom (War Advertising Council)

"The most important thing in communication is hearing what isn't said."

— Peter Drucker

"We have two ears and one mouth so that we can listen twice as much as we speak."

— Epictetus

"Attention is the rarest and purest form of generosity."

— Simone Weil

"The art of conversation is the art of hearing as well as of being heard."

- William Hazlitt

"What we see depends mainly on what we look for."

— John Lubbock

"In the age of information, ignorance is a choice."

— Donny Miller

"The greatest gift you can give someone is your undivided attention."

— Jim Rohn

"Sometimes, you need to step outside, get some air, and remind yourself of who you are and who you want to be."

— Anonymous

"The quieter you become, the more you can hear."

— Ram Dass

Bible Verses:

"Wise people don't make a show of their knowledge, but fools broadcast their foolishness."
-Proverbs 12:23 (NLT)

"Watch your tongue and keep your mouth shut, and you will stay out of trouble."
-Proverbs 21:23 (NLT)

"Even fools are thought wise when they keep silent; with their mouths shut, they seem intelligent."
-Proverbs 17:28 (NLT)

"Yet God has made everything beautiful for its own time. He has planted eternity in the human heart, but even so, people cannot see the whole scope of God's work from beginning to end."
-Ecclesiastes 3:11 (NLT)

"Understand this, my dear brothers and sisters: You must all be quick to listen, slow to speak, and slow to get angry."
-James 1:19 (NLT)

"Spouting off before listening to the facts is both shameful and foolish."
-Proverbs 18:13 (NLT)

"Let the wise listen to these proverbs and become even wiser. Let those with understanding receive guidance."
-Proverbs 1:5 (NLT)

"Though good advice lies deep within the heart, a person with understanding will draw it out."
-Proverbs 20:5 (NLT)

"A time to tear and a time to mend. A time to be quiet and a time to speak."
-Ecclesiastes 3:7 (NLT)

"A prudent person foresees danger and takes precautions. The simpleton goes blindly on and suffers the consequences."
-Proverbs 27:12 (NLT)

"Stay alert! Watch out for your great enemy, the devil. He prowls around like a roaring lion, looking for someone to devour."
-1 Peter 5:8 (NLT)

"The heavens proclaim the glory of God. The skies display his craftsmanship."
-Psalm 19:1 (NLT)

"And now, dear brothers and sisters, one final thing. Fix your thoughts on what is true,

and honorable, and right, and pure, and lovely, and admirable. Think about things that are excellent and worthy of praise."
-Philippians 4:8 (NLT)

Today's Affirmations:

- I listen with intent, understanding the value of both spoken and unspoken words.
- I observe and learn from every experience, both positive and negative.
- I use my ears and eyes twice as much as I use my mouth, seeking wisdom in silence.
- I pay attention to my surroundings, ensuring my safety and staying vigilant.
- I guard my words, knowing that wisdom is found in restraint.
- I trust my discernment, recognizing when someone reveals their true character.
- I stay present and fully engaged in the moment, undistracted by technology.
- I take time to appreciate the beauty of God's creation in nature and the world around me.
- I honor the wisdom in listening more and speaking less, gaining insight with every observation.
- I walk with awareness and purpose, confident in God's protection and guidance.

with love,
Dad

GRAND RISING DAY EIGHT

STAY PURPOSEFUL AND PRODUCTIVE!

"The devil finds work for idle hands; an idle mind is the devil's playground."

Being lazy may seem easy and comfortable at first, but it ultimately complicates life and opens the door for the devil to tempt, use, and embarrass you. My personal experience serves as a cautionary tale; I neglected my fitness for years, and in doing so, I paid a heavy price. I became overweight, developed high blood pressure, and found myself on the verge of diabetes.

Regaining my health required extreme effort and dedication, and I realized that it's far easier to maintain your health than to try to repair and restore it after neglect.

I firmly believe that hard work sets you apart from the competition, as many people wrongly assume that success will come easily. In sports, the athletes who appear to play effortlessly are often the ones who have put in the most work and honed their skills. Take, for instance, the late great Kobe Bryant, the Black Mamba himself. He once said, "Mamba mentality is all about focusing on the process and trusting in the hard work when it matters most.

It's the ultimate mantra for the competitive spirit."[4] However, I also believe that being ambitiously lazy can be beneficial. This concept represents the mother of invention and efficiency. An "ambitiously lazy" person is driven to achieve their goals but prefers the most efficient, least effort-intensive ways to do so. They strive to accomplish a lot while exerting minimal effort, using innovative solutions to maximize productivity.

I have a friend who faced challenges in his marriage. While he was doing well financially, he was searching for a better career opportunity. When he sought help updating his resume, his next-door neighbor—a married woman—offered assistance. They set a date to work on the resume, but when he arrived, her husband was not home. She offered him a few drinks, and they quickly veered into conversations about their respective marital issues. Unfortunately, instead of leaving, he stayed and ended up making a mistake that ultimately led to the demise of his marriage.

My intention is not to judge his actions, but to emphasize the importance of living above reproach. He should have left as soon as he realized her husband was absent. Idleness and failing to set boundaries can easily lead to unnecessary downfalls.

Quotes:

"Without discipline, no matter how talented you are, you're nothing."
— Mike Tyson

"Be the hardest working person you can be. That's how you separate yourself from the competition."
— Stephen Curry

"Discipline is the bridge between goals and accomplishment."
— Jim Rohn

"Nothing will work unless you do."
— Maya Angelou

"The idle man does not see the devil's work."
— Blaise Pascal

"Early to Bed Early to rise makes a man healthy, wealthy and wise…"
- Benjamin Franklin (Poor Richard's Almanack)

"Laziness is nothing more than the habit of resting before you are tired."
— Jules Renard

"Curiosity, rationalization, and laziness are no match against courage, self control and mental toughness."

— John Blytheway

"Laziness is a secret ingredient that goes into failure, but it's only kept a secret from the person who fails."

— Robert Half

"Motivation is when your dreams put on work clothes."

— Benjamin Franklin

"I can't relate to lazy people. We don't speak the same language. I don't understand you."

— Kobe Bryant

"Hard work WORKS!"

— Denzel Washington

"Genius is one percent inspiration and ninety-nine percent perspiration."

— Thomas Edison

Bible Verses:

"Lazy people want much but get little, but those who work hard will prosper."
-Proverbs 13:4 (NLT)

"Those too lazy to plow in the right season will have no food at the harvest."
-Proverbs 20:4 (NLT)

"Lazy people are soon poor; hard workers get rich."
-Proverbs 10:4 (NLT)

"Work hard and become a leader; be lazy and become a slave."
-Proverbs 12:24 (NLT)

"Laziness leads to a sagging roof; idleness leads to a leaky house."
-Ecclesiastes 10:18 (NLT)

"Work willingly at whatever you do, as though you were working for the Lord rather than for people. Remember that the Lord will give you an inheritance as your reward, and that the master you are serving is Christ."
-Colossians 3:23-24 (NLT)

"Even while we were with you, we gave you this command: 'Those unwilling to work will not get to eat.'"
-2 Thessalonians 3:10 (NLT)

"Despite their desires, the lazy will come to ruin, for their hands refuse to work."
-Proverbs 21:25 (NLT)

"So let's not get tired of doing what is good. At just the right time we will reap a harvest of blessing if we don't give up."
-Galatians 6:9 (NLT)

Today's Affirmation:

- I reject laziness and embrace diligence to build a stronger, healthier future.
- I am disciplined, staying active and focused to avoid the temptations of idleness.
- Hard work and dedication set me apart and lead to success.
- I maintain my health through consistent effort, knowing it's easier to sustain than to repair.
- I find efficient and innovative ways to reach my goals with minimal wasted effort.
- I live with integrity and avoid situations that compromise my values.
- I stay productive and make the most of every opportunity.
- My ambitions are driven by purpose, and I achieve them through smart and focused work.
- I am not idle; I use my time wisely to accomplish great things.
- Hard work works, and I trust the process to lead me to success.

with love,
Dad

GRAND RISING DAY NINE

CHOOSE YOUR FRIENDS AND YOUR ASSOCIATIONS WISELY.

Have you ever stopped to think about how much your circle influences your life? Who you spend time with shapes the person you eventually become. Your associations can elevate you as much as they can bring you down. I always want to know who my kids are hanging out with, and I like to know their parents as well. The fruit doesn't fall far from the tree. I learned this lesson from my mother, who would often ask—some might say "be nosey"—about my friends and whereabouts. I thought she was being intrusive when I was younger, but as my mother she had every right to be involved in ALL of my business.

Growing up in a small town in Florida called LaBelle, there's an area nicknamed "the quarters." It wasn't the best-kept place; while there were nice people, it was also known for many negative situations. My parents always warned me to stay away, or I would face consequences. (They were old-school, believing in the saying, "spare the rod, spoil the child.") For the most part, I listened because I didn't want to get into trouble or face the wrath of my VERY spirited Jamaican parents.

One of my mentors used to say you will become the average of the five people you hang out with. If you surround yourself with four soccer players, guess what you'll likely start liking or watching? Soccer. If you spend time with four millionaires, you will probably become the fifth one. Similarly, if you hang out with people who have a cold or are sick, you're likely to catch a cold or get sick.

This brings me to another important point: the crab mentality. This metaphor illustrates the mindset that says, "If I can't have it, neither can you." You don't want to surround yourself with those types of people; they will pull you down when you're trying to rise. While they may not vocalize it, your success shines a light on their lack of ambition or achievements.

Instead, seek out high achievers—people who will uplift you and propel you to greater heights. Consider individuals who inspire you or who have overcome challenges to achieve their goals. Surrounding yourself with such influences can not only motivate you but also create a supportive environment for personal growth.

As you navigate your journey, remember that your associations can either be stepping stones to success or stumbling blocks. Choose wisely! Who are the five people you spend the most time with, and how are they influencing your journey?

Quotes:

"Some people get their worth from hanging with losers... they become self-proclaimed encouragers, not realizing they are just sinking down in the same pit in the process."

— Ashley Shaw (My wise wife)

"You are the company you keep."

— Ivy Shaw (My mother)

"If you are the smartest person in the room, then you are in the wrong room."

— Confucius

"You are the average of the five people you spend the most time with."

— Jim Rohn

"Friends are angels who lift us up to our feet when our own wings have trouble remembering how to fly!"

— Oprah

"Surround yourself with only people who are going to lift you higher. Life is already filled with those who want to bring you down."
— Oprah

"A true friend knows your weaknesses, but shows you your strengths; feels your fears, but fortifies your faith; sees your anxieties, but frees your spirit; recognizes your disabilities, but emphasizes your possibilities."
— William Arthur Ward

"Life is like an elevator. On your way up, sometimes you have to stop and let some people off."
— Ziad K. Abdelnour

"Your friends are like elevators, they either take you up or they take you down. We become who we surround ourselves with."
— Anonymous

"I am a part of all that I have met."
— Excerpt from Alfred Lord Tennyson's poem *Ulysses*

Bible Verses:

"Walk with the wise and become wise; associate with fools and get in trouble."
-Proverbs 13:20 (NLT)

"Beware of false prophets, who come to you in sheep's clothing, but inwardly they are ravenous wolves. You will know them by their fruits. Do men gather grapes from thornbushes or figs from thistles? Even so, every good tree bears good fruit, but a bad tree bears bad fruit. A good tree cannot bear bad fruit, nor can a bad tree bear good fruit. Every tree that does not bear good fruit is cut down and thrown into the fire. Therefore by their fruits you will know them.
-Matthew 7:15-20 (NKJV)

"The godly give good advice to their friends; the wicked lead them astray."
-Proverbs 12:26 (NLT)

"Don't be fooled by those who say such things, for "bad company corrupts good character."
-1 Corinthians 15:33 (NLT)

"As iron sharpens iron, so a friend sharpens a friend."
-Proverbs 27:17 (NLT)

"Don't befriend angry people or associate with hot-tempered people, or you will learn to be like them and endanger your soul."
-Proverbs 22:24-25 (NLT)

> "Two people are better off than one, for they can help each other succeed. If one person falls, the other can reach out and help. But someone who falls alone is in real trouble."
> -Ecclesiastes 4:9-10 (NLT)

> "Oh, the joys of those who do not follow the advice of the wicked, or stand around with sinners, or join in with mockers. But they delight in the law of the Lord, meditating on it day and night."
> -Psalm 1:1-2 (NLT)

Today's Affirmations:

- I choose my friends and associations carefully, knowing they shape my future.
- I surround myself with people who lift me higher and inspire me to grow.
- I seek out friends who challenge me to be better and sharpen my character.
- I distance myself from negativity and those who try to pull me down.
- I value friendships that push me toward success and higher achievements.
- I am intentional about the company I keep, associating with those who align with my values.
- I attract and maintain relationships with wise, ambitious, and positive people.
- I am a positive influence in the lives of others, encouraging growth and success.
- I am part of a community that fosters success and personal development.
- I elevate myself by walking with the wise and avoiding those who lead me astray

with love,
Dad

GRAND RISING DAY TEN

Choose Your Hard

When my mother, Ivy Shaw, and my father, Junior Shaw, passed away in the same year, just months apart, it was one of the roughest periods of my life. My mother had been battling cancer, and we knew her time was short. Then, unexpectedly, my father suffered a brain aneurysm and passed away before her. Losing them both so closely was devastating, but I made it through, thanks in large part to my loving and caring wife, Ashley.

I was fortunate to have deep conversations with both my mother and father before they ever became sick. Some great mentors taught me the value of appreciation and gratitude, and I made it a point to apply those lessons with my parents, knowing they wouldn't be around forever. No one is ever truly "prepared" for the loss of a parent. Everyone experiences it differently, but one thing that helped me was the self-development I had invested in over the years.

By the time I faced this loss, I had gained a level of emotional stability. Because I'd had those hard, uncomfortable conversations with my parents, I found peace knowing they understood how much I loved and appreciated them. I even wrote my mother a "love letter," sharing how the values she instilled in me had taken root and shaped my life. (Some examples of the values she instilled into me are shared in Grand Rising, Day 4.)

Two years to the day of my mother's passing, my brother had a stroke. Seeing him on life support—the brother I always looked up to, once my hero—was incredibly tough. Thankfully, he has since recovered. I'm truly grateful to have the Lord by my side, and a strong, supportive wife who stands with me through every challenge. During this season, Ashley was a pillar of support. She allowed me to cry, grieve, and express myself in ways I couldn't with anyone else. Her grace, understanding, and care reminded me of how blessed I am to call her not just my wife, but also my best friend and confidante. During those difficult times, one Bible verse I held onto was James 1:2-4 (NLT):

"Dear brothers and sisters, when troubles of any kind come your way, consider it an opportunity for great joy. For you know that when your faith is tested, your endurance has a chance to grow. So let it grow, for when your endurance is fully developed, you will be perfect and complete, needing nothing."

This verse was a lifeline for me. At first, the idea of "counting it all joy" seemed impossible in the face of such profound loss. But as I reflected on those words, I realized that the trials I faced were shaping me into a stronger, more grounded person. Losing my parents taught me how short and precious our time on earth truly is. It pushed me to focus on what truly matters—accomplishing the things God has called me to do and making a meaningful difference not only in my life but in the lives of others.

That season of grief became a season of growth. It taught me endurance and perseverance. I began to see my parents' legacy not as something lost, but as something to carry forward. The strength I gained through those trials was not just for me—it was so I could uplift others and make the most of the time I've been given.

Thank God for His words of encouragement and wisdom.
I also want to share an excerpt from Pastor Keith Craft that blessed me. He speaks powerfully about choosing to overcome the hard things in life, and I hope it blesses you as much as it has blessed me.

CHOOSE YOUR HARD!

Being your best is hard
Being your normal is hard
Making wise decisions is hard
Making bad decisions is hard
Being in shape is hard
Being out of shape is hard
Losing weight is hard
Being fat is hard
Working out is hard
Being weak is hard
Being disciplined is hard
Being lazy is hard
Getting out of your comfort zone is hard
Staying in your comfort zone is hard
Starting a business is hard
Working for someone else is hard
Making a lot of money is hard
Making a little bit of money is hard
Being rich is hard
Being poor is hard
Having great relationships is hard
Having bad relationships is hard
Having friends is hard
Having no friends is hard
Fighting for your marriage is hard
Divorce is hard
Having a lot of things is hard
Having nothing is hard
Living on purpose is hard
Living off purpose is hard
Doing life God's way is hard
Doing life your own way is hard
Everything is hard!
Choose your hard!

-Keith Craft[5]

Quotes:

"Do not pray for easy lives. Pray to be stronger men. Do not pray for tasks equal to your powers. Pray for powers equal to your tasks. Then the doing of your work shall be no miracle, but you shall be the miracle."

— Reverend Phillips Brooks

"The obstacle is the way!"

— Ryan Holiday

"Hard times create strong men. Strong men create good times. Good times create weak men. And, weak men create hard times."

— G. Michael Hopf

"Adversity causes some men to break; others to break records."

— William Arthur Ward

"Life is 10% what happens to us and 90% how we react to it."

— Charles R. Swindoll

"You may have to fight a battle more than once to win it."

— Margaret Thatcher

"The greater the obstacle, the more glory in overcoming it."

— Molière

"The only way out is through."

— Robert Frost

"We must embrace pain and burn it as fuel for our journey."

— Kenji Miyazawa

"It's not the load that breaks you down, it's the way you carry it."

— Lou Holtz

"Difficulties in life are intended to make us better, not bitter."

— Dan Reeves

"Success is not final, failure is not fatal: It is the courage to continue that counts."

— Winston Churchill

"Hardships often prepare ordinary people for an extraordinary destiny."

— C.S. Lewis

"Strength does not come from winning. Your struggles develop your strengths. When you go through hardships and decide not to surrender, that is strength."

— Arnold Schwarzenegger

Bible Verses:

"Dear brothers and sisters, when troubles of any kind come your way, consider it an opportunity for great joy. For you know that when your faith is tested, your endurance has a chance to grow. So let it grow, for when your endurance is fully developed, you will be perfect and complete, needing nothing."

-James 1:2-4 (NLT)

"For I can do everything through Christ, who gives me strength."

-Philippians 4:13 (NLT)

"We can rejoice, too, when we run into problems and trials, for we know that they help us develop endurance. And endurance develops strength of character, and character strengthens our confident hope of salvation. And this hope will not lead to disappointment."

-Romans 5:3-5 (NLT)

"But those who trust in the Lord will find new strength. They will soar high on wings like eagles. They will run and not grow weary. They will walk and not faint."

-Isaiah 40:31 (NLT)

"In his kindness, God called you to share in his eternal glory by means of Christ Jesus. So after you have suffered a little while, he will restore, support, and strengthen you, and he will place you on a firm foundation."

-1 Peter 5:10

"For our present troubles are small and won't last very long. Yet they produce for us a glory that vastly outweighs them and will last forever!"

-2 Corinthians 4:17

"Trust in the Lord with all your heart; do not depend on your own understanding. Seek his will in all you do, and he will show you which path to take."

-Proverbs 3:5-6

"Then Jesus said, 'Come to me, all of you who are weary and carry heavy burdens, and I will give you rest. Take my yoke upon you. Let me teach you, because I am humble and gentle at heart, and you will find rest for your souls. For my yoke is easy to bear, and the burden I give you is light.'"

-Matthew 11:28-30

Today's Affirmations:

- I embrace challenges, knowing they make me stronger.
- I choose to overcome hard things with resilience and faith.
- I face adversity with courage, trusting in God's plan for my life.
- I make wise decisions, even when they are tough.

- I am disciplined and committed to living my best life.
- I choose progress over comfort and growth over stagnation.
- I can do all things through Christ who strengthens me.
- I thrive under pressure and rise above difficult circumstances.
- I choose my hard and trust that it will lead to greater rewards.
- I am a conqueror; no challenge is too great for me with God by my side.

with love,
Dad

GRAND RISING DAY ELEVEN

Guard Your Heart: Break Free From Hate and Animosity

I mentioned in GRAND RISING DAY 2 that early in my business career, I had people in my life who turned out to be untrustworthy and unscrupulous. For years, I harbored hate and resentment in my heart toward them. This, combined with the stress of my parents' passing and financial pressures, eventually landed me in the hospital.

Because we had invested so much time and energy with these people, I couldn't understand why they betrayed us. I would constantly talk about how bad and evil they were instead of letting go and moving forward. What I didn't realize at the time was that while I was consumed by the past, they had likely long forgotten about what they had done. The hate and animosity I held onto began to destroy my attitude, my health, my relationships, and it stole my joy and happiness.

At one point, I realized that the situation—and, in essence, they—were controlling me because I couldn't let it go. My wife helped me see this. She said, "You talk about what they did to us every day in some shape or form. I can't wait until this is no longer a topic in our household." This was a turning point. I hadn't even realized how consumed I was by everything that had happened or that I was bringing it up daily.

Then, the Lord placed it on my heart to start praying for them. So that's what I did. I began praying for their healing, that they would grow and become better people. I prayed for the Lord to bless them in every area of their lives. What I discovered was profound: it's hard to continue hating someone when you're sincerely praying for blessings over their life.

I also came to realize that hurting people hurt people. Somewhere in their lives, they were hurting, and that's why they chose to hurt us. Through this process, I found healing.

So, is there someone in your life that you are harboring hate or animosity toward? Is it your father for not being in your life, or not fulfilling the role you thought he should? Is it toward your mother, a sibling, or a former best friend? Start praying for those who have hurt you and begin the journey of forgiveness. It will be transformative for your healing.

Quotes:

"To forgive is to set a prisoner free and discover that the prisoner was you."
— Lewis B. Smedes

"The best revenge is to be unlike him who performed the injury."
— Marcus Aurelius

"Darkness cannot drive out darkness; only light can do that. Hate cannot drive out hate; only love can do that."
— Martin Luther King Jr.

"Holding onto anger is like drinking poison and expecting the other person to die."
— Buddha

"The weak can never forgive. Forgiveness is the attribute of the strong."
— Mahatma Gandhi

"An eye for an eye will only make the whole world blind."
— Mahatma Gandhi

"Forgiveness is not something we do for other people. We do it for ourselves to get well and move on."
— Unknown

"Forgive others, not because they deserve forgiveness, but because you deserve peace."
— Jonathan Lockwood Huie

"When you forgive, you heal. When you let go, you grow."

— Unknown

"Letting go gives us freedom, and freedom is the only condition for happiness."

— Thich Nhat Hanh

Bible Verses:

"But I say, love your enemies! Pray for those who persecute you! In that way, you will be acting as true children of your Father in heaven. For he gives his sunlight to both the evil and the good, and he sends rain on the just and the unjust alike. If you love only those who love you, what reward is there for that? Even corrupt tax collectors do that much. If you are kind only to your friends, how are you different from anyone else? Even pagans do that. But you are to be perfect, even as your Father in heaven is perfect."

-Matthew 5:44-48 (NLT)

"But when you are praying, first forgive anyone you are holding a grudge against, so that your Father in heaven will forgive your sins, too."

-Mark 11:25 (NLT)

"Dear friends, never take revenge. Leave that to the righteous anger of God. For the Scriptures say, 'I will take revenge; I will pay them back,' says the Lord. Instead, 'If your enemies are hungry, feed them. If they are thirsty, give them something to drink. In doing this, you will heap burning coals of shame on their heads.' Don't let evil conquer you, but conquer evil by doing good."

-Romans 12:19-21 (NLT)

"Bear with each other and forgive one another if any of you has a grievance against someone. Forgive as the Lord forgave you. And over all these virtues put on love, which binds them all together in perfect unity."

-Colossians 3:13-14 (NIV)

"Love your enemies! Do good to them. Lend to them without expecting to be repaid. Then your reward from heaven will be very great, and you will truly be acting as children of the Most High, for he is kind to those who are unthankful and wicked. You must be compassionate, just as your Father is compassionate."

-Luke 6:35-36 (NLT)

"Work at living in peace with everyone, and work at living a holy life, for those who are not holy will not see the Lord. Look after each other so that none of you fails to receive the grace of God. Watch out that no poisonous root of bitterness grows up to trouble you, corrupting many."

-Hebrews 12:14-15 (NLT)

"Get rid of all bitterness, rage, anger, harsh words, and slander, as well as all types of evil behavior. Instead, be kind to each other, tenderhearted, forgiving one another, just as God through Christ has forgiven you."
-Ephesians 4:31-32 (NLT)

"If you forgive those who sin against you, your heavenly Father will forgive you. But if you refuse to forgive others, your Father will not forgive your sins."
-Matthew 6:14-15 (NLT)

"Make allowance for each other's faults, and forgive anyone who offends you. Remember, the Lord forgave you, so you must forgive others."
-Colossians 3:13 (NLT)

"But to you who are willing to listen, I say, love your enemies! Do good to those who hate you. Bless those who curse you. Pray for those who hurt you."
-Luke 6:27-28 (NLT)

"Hatred stirs up quarrels, but love makes up for all offenses."
-Proverbs 10:12 (NLT)

Today's Affirmations:

- I release bitterness and choose forgiveness, just as God forgives me.
- I am free from unforgiveness and blessed with peace in my heart.
- I embrace grace and forgive others, healing my soul.
- I choose to love and pray for those who hurt me.
- I trust God for justice and overcome evil by doing good.
- My heart is filled with love, not hate, and I release all animosity.
- I forgive others and open myself to God's blessings and peace.
- I live in peace, free from the bitterness of resentment.
- I let go of the past, finding healing through prayer and forgiveness.
- I choose forgiveness and peace, letting go of what no longer serves me.

with love,
Dad

GRAND RISING DAY TWELVE

Do NOT Worry, God's Got You!
(Be Anxious For Nothing/Keep Your Stress Levels Low)

Being anxious and stressed can raise your blood pressure and cortisol levels. Our family has a history of high blood pressure and heart issues (which I rebuke in the name of Jesus!). I once lived a contentious and very argumentative lifestyle, similar to what I saw growing up with my parents. (ask my wife), I used to blame my parents for my attitude and my actions... However, I no longer blame them for my attitude or my actions. Since moving out and maturing, I've realized that I have the power to choose who I want to be. While my parents influenced me, from 0-18 while I was living under their roof, it was still ultimately my decision to act with anger and spite. Now as I have grown older and wiser and have learned from trusted mentors, I now understand that I have the ability to create a more peaceful environment for myself and my young, impressionable family.

Even still... Controlling stress levels is very important for your long-term health. It is advantageous to get some good rest, exercise, eat healthy and take care of your mental health.

"High levels of cortisol from long-term stress can increase your risk of heart disease by raising your blood pressure, blood sugar, triglycerides, and blood cholesterol. These are all common risk factors for heart disease. Stress can also cause plaque deposits to build up in your arteries, and it can affect how your blood clots, making it stickier and increasing your risk of stroke."

-University of Rochester Medical Center[6]

Medical Reviewers:
- Callie Tayrien, RN MSN
- Stacey Wojcik, MBA BSN RN
- Steven Kang, MD

The Stoic philosopher Epictetus teaches the importance of focusing on what is within our control and letting go of what is not. "Make the best use of what is in your power, and take the rest as it happens." His belief is that we should not worry about things beyond our control, but rather focus on our own actions and responses.

Why am I telling you this? Because the Bible says in Philippians 4:6-7, "*Be anxious for nothing, but in everything by prayer and supplication, with thanksgiving, let your requests be made known to God; and the peace of God, which surpasses all understanding, will guard your hearts and minds through Christ Jesus.*"

Quotes:

"Anxiety does not empty tomorrow of its sorrows, but only empties today of its strength."

— Charles Spurgeon

"Do not anticipate trouble or worry about what may never happen. Keep in the sunlight."

— Benjamin Franklin

"Anxiety is a thin stream of fear trickling through the mind. If encouraged, it cuts a channel into which all other thoughts are drained."

— Arthur Somers Roche

"Present fears are less than horrible imaginings."

— William Shakespeare

"Nothing diminishes anxiety faster than action."

— Walter Anderson

"When you know you already won nothing else matters"

— Toby Ayers

Bible Verses:

"Anxiety in the heart of man causes depression, But a good word makes it glad."
-Proverbs 12:25 (NKJV)

"Be anxious for nothing, but in everything by prayer and supplication, with thanksgiving, let your requests be made known to God; and the peace of God, which surpasses all understanding, will guard your hearts and minds through Christ Jesus. Finally, brethren, whatever things are true, whatever things are noble, whatever things are just, whatever things are pure, whatever things are lovely, whatever things are of good report, if there is any virtue and if there is anything praiseworthy—meditate on these things."
-Philippians 4:6-8 (NKJV)

"The Lord is my shepherd; I shall not want. He makes me to lie down in green pastures; He leads me beside the still waters. He restores my soul; He leads me in the paths of righteousness For His name's sake. Yea, though I walk through the valley of the shadow of death, I will fear no evil; For You are with me; Your rod and Your staff, they comfort me. You prepare a table before me in the presence of my enemies; You anoint my head with oil; My cup runs over. Surely goodness and mercy shall follow me All the days of my life; And I will dwell in the house of the Lord Forever."
-Psalms 23:1-6 (NKJV)

Today's Affirmations:

- I release all anxiety and trust in God's perfect plan for my life.
- I am too blessed to be stressed!
- God's peace guards my heart and mind through Christ Jesus.
- I take positive action, and action cures fear.
- I choose to live in peace, free from worry and anxiety.
- I control my attitude and my reactions, creating a calm environment.
- The Lord is my Shepherd; I have everything I need.
- I focus on what is pure, noble, and good, and I find strength in God's Word.
- I rest in the assurance that God is with me in every situation.
- My heart is filled with joy, and I live without fear of the future.

with love,
Dad

GRAND RISING
DAY THIRTEEN

BE OPEN TO CRITICISM FROM THOSE YOU TRUST

Invite criticism from friends; then when it comes from your enemies, you will be broken in. There is a huge importance of accepting criticism constructively and understanding its role in personal and professional growth. Solomon said, "If you accept correction, you will be honored." Charlie Shedd, American pastor, Christian family life author, and counselor gives us ten ways to grow through criticism:

1. Criticism is often a compliment. The barbs in daily life strike only those who raise their heads above ground level. Jesus said, *"Count yourself blessed every time someone cuts you down…it means that the truth is too close for comfort and that that person is uncomfortable"* (Lk. 6:22 MSG).
2. Accept that you have faults which are open to censure. Stay humble, and criticism won't rattle you.
3. *"The words of the godly save lives"* (Prov. 12:6 NLT). Invite criticism from friends; then when it comes from your enemies, you will be broken in.
4. Let criticism make you better. When you burn with anger, you destroy the passport to your own improvement. *"When you do right and suffer for it… take it patiently"* (1Pet. 2:20 RSV).
5. Some criticism should be ignored, especially if it stems from false motives. Never give unhappy people the key to your happiness, the person

who belittles you; they are only trying to cut you down to their size.
6. Keep it in perspective. Everybody hasn't heard. Most people don't care. One bad word doesn't cancel the good in you.
7. Let criticism make you kinder. Remind yourself that you have criticized others too. Is this a boomerang that started in your own heart?
8. Pray for your critics. It will improve them and neutralize your bitterness. Hate destroys your health and steals your happiness.
9. Check with the Master Critic. What does God say? How do things look deep in your soul?
10. When you have checked to make sure you're right, move ahead. In quiet confidence finish what you started, because God's promises are to those who endure (See Heb. 6:12).

Quotes:

"Criticism may not be agreeable, but it is necessary. It fulfills the same function as pain in the human body. It calls attention to an unhealthy state of things."
— Winston Churchill

"Do what you feel in your heart to be right, for you'll be criticized anyway."
— Eleanor Roosevelt

"The final proof of greatness lies in being able to endure criticism without resentment."
— Elbert Hubbard

"The trouble with most of us is that we would rather be ruined by praise than saved by criticism."
— Norman Vincent Peale

"If you have no critics, you'll likely have no success."
— Malcolm X

"Criticism is something we can avoid easily by saying nothing, doing nothing, and being nothing."

"Listen with the intent to understand, not the intent to reply."
— Stephen R. Covey

Bible Verses:

"If you ignore criticism, you will end in poverty and disgrace; if you accept correction, you will be honored."
-Proverbs 13:18 (NLT)

"If you listen to constructive criticism, you will be at home among the wise."
-Proverbs 15:31 (NLT)

"So don't bother correcting mockers; they will only hate you. But correct the wise, and they will love you."
-Proverbs 9:8 (NLT)

"A single rebuke does more for a person of understanding than a hundred lashes on the back of a fool."
-Proverbs 17:10 (NLT)

"Wounds from a sincere friend are better than many kisses from an enemy."
-Proverbs 27:6 (NLT)

Today's Affirmations:

- I accept criticism as an opportunity for growth and improvement.
- I am open to feedback and use it to become stronger and wiser.
- I choose to focus on what I believe is right, regardless of others' opinions.
- I understand that criticism is a natural part of success and growth.
- I have the strength to endure criticism without losing confidence or self-worth.
- I stay true to myself, even when facing criticism from others.
- I embrace constructive criticism as a tool to refine my abilities and character.
- I am grateful for those who offer feedback with the intention of helping me improve.
- I can differentiate between constructive feedback and destructive criticism.
- I remain calm and composed in the face of criticism, knowing it is a part of my journey to greatness.

with love,
Dad

GRAND RISING DAY FOURTEEN

Control Your Words

The words we use are either a powerful creative force or a destructive one, depending on how we choose to use them. Proverbs 18:21 (NKJV) tells us: *"Death and life are in the power of the tongue, and those who love it will eat its fruit."*

My wife and I are very intentional about the words we speak over our family and especially our children. There was a moment when my wife had a crucial conversation with her mother about some phrases she often used while raising her, phrases that might have seemed harmless but carried unintended weight. She gently explained that while those words may have been common in the past, they weren't the kind of words we wanted spoken over our son. For example, she would sometimes say things like, "You're being so bad," or "You always act up," without realizing the negative impact.

My mother-in-law (whom we lovingly call "Gigi" because she's truly amazing and too fly to be called grandma) meant no harm. These were phrases passed down from her own upbringing. However, we wanted to ensure that the words spoken over our son would build him up.

When our son misbehaves, we are careful not to label him as a "bad kid." Instead, we remind him that he is a good child who is simply acting out of character. We speak life and God's truth over him, affirming his potential.

We prayed for him to be a leader, to be bold, confident, and even for him to be left-handed—God has blessed him with all these traits. We firmly believe that our faithfulness and the words we speak have shaped him.

"The tongue has the power of life and death, and those who love it will eat its fruits."

— Proverbs 18:21

This proverb encourages us to handle our words with responsibility, knowing that each one plants seeds that will bear fruit. As believers, we are called to speak life-giving words—words that reflect God's grace, offer encouragement, inspire hope, and affirm faith. In doing so, we not only uplift others but also partake in the fruits of righteousness and love.

Prayer:

Heavenly Father,

In the stillness of this new morning, I stand before You, recognizing the immense power You've placed in my words. I ask for the wisdom to wield this power with grace, the restraint to refrain from harm, and the vision to see the impact of every word I utter.

Grant me, O Lord, the discernment to speak life into dry places, to use my voice for healing where there is hurt, and for encouragement where there is despair. May my tongue be an instrument of Your peace, speaking truth wrapped in love, sowing seeds of Your goodness in every conversation.

As I move through this day, let my words be a reflection of Your heart—full of life, full of love, full of You. Should I falter, gently correct me, for it is my desire to eat the fruit of life-giving speech, sharing the bounty with those You place in my path.

In the precious and life-affirming name of Jesus, I pray, Amen.

Quotes:

"This is huge! We are big on controlling our words in our family. Not only ours but the words spoken over us/our family. It takes effort/mindfulness, but I believe it helps us function at a higher level. It also makes us more effective leaders as we're able to affirm, even in moments of correction or redirection."

— Ashley Shaw, (Quote during a time frame when we led a young adults group at church)

Bible Verses:

"The tongue can bring death or life; those who love to talk will reap the consequences."
-Proverbs 18:21 (NLT)

"Don't use foul or abusive language. Let everything you say be good and helpful, so that your words will be an encouragement to those who hear them."
-Ephesians 4:29

"In the same way, the tongue is a small thing that makes grand speeches. But a tiny spark can set a great forest on fire. And among all the parts of the body, the tongue is a flame of fire. It is a whole world of wickedness, corrupting your entire body. It can set your whole life on fire, for it is set on fire by hell itself."
-James 3:5-6

"Gentle words are a tree of life; a deceitful tongue crushes the spirit."
-Proverbs 15:4

"And I tell you this, you must give an account on judgment day for every idle word you speak. The words you say will either acquit you or condemn you."
-Matthew 12:36-37

"Some people make cutting remarks, but the words of the wise bring healing."
-Proverbs 12:18

"Let your conversation be gracious and attractive so that you will have the right response for everyone."
-Colossians 4:6

"May the words of my mouth and the meditation of my heart be pleasing to you, O Lord, my rock and my redeemer."
-Psalm 19:14

"Kind words are like honey—sweet to the soul and healthy for the body."
-Proverbs 16:24

Today's Affirmations:

- I control my words with wisdom and care.
- My words are a creative force for good.
- I speak life and positivity over my family and myself.
- I choose words that reflect God's truth and love.
- My speech uplifts, encourages, and inspires.

LEGACY OF WISDOM

- I am mindful of the power my words hold.
- I use my voice to plant seeds of hope and faith.
- I affirm the goodness in others, even in correction.
- My words reflect the grace and love of God.
- I speak blessings over my life and the lives of others.

with love,
Dad

GRAND RISING DAY FIFTEEN

KEEP HOPE ALIVE!

Be inspired to keep hope alive, even in challenging times.
Hope is a strong and confident expectation! Without hope the heart grows weary. Hope gives you courage, hope gives you life.
The Lord says in Jeremiah 29:11 (NLT):
"For I know the plans I have for you," says the Lord. "They are plans for good and not for disaster, to give you a future and a hope."

I would like to use one of the most famous examples in history (outside of Jesus) of a leader giving hope to his followers in history is Sir Winston Churchill.

Sir Winston Churchill (1874-1965) was the Prime Minister of the United Kingdom during World War II. He served as the Prime Minister from 1940-1945 and again from 1951-1955. He is most famous for leading Britain through WWII, inspiring the nation with his speeches and helping to forge the Allied Victory.

Winston Churchill delivered the famous "We Shall Fight on the Beaches" speech on June 4, 1940, to inspire, give hope and rally the British people during one of the most challenging moments of World War II. The speech followed the evacuation of over 300,000 British and Allied troops from Dunkirk, France, as they narrowly escaped capture by the advancing German forces. Though the evacuation was a success, it was still a major military setback, as much of Europe had fallen under Nazi control, and the threat of a German invasion of Britain seemed imminent.

Churchill gave the speech to:

- Reassure the nation: Despite the dire circumstances, Churchill wanted to maintain national morale, assuring the British people that the fight was far from over.
- Prepare for the worst: He acknowledged the possibility of a German invasion but made it clear that Britain would resist with all its strength.
- Inspire resolve and defiance: Churchill's words conveyed that Britain would continue fighting on land, sea, and air, using all means necessary to protect the homeland.
- Unify the country: The speech was a call to action, aimed at uniting the British people in their determination to defend their country, regardless of the obstacles.

This speech marked a turning point in Britain's resolve, symbolizing their steadfastness to fight against the Nazis, even when standing alone. Winston Churchill's most famous speech that gave hope to his country was his "We Shall Fight on the Beaches" speech, delivered on June 4, 1940. This speech came at a critical moment during World War II, after the British Army's evacuation from Dunkirk, where Allied forces had faced a significant setback.

In this speech, Churchill acknowledged the dire situation but reinforced Britain's resolve to fight on. He spoke of defending the country at all costs, vowing never to surrender, regardless of the odds. The speech included these stirring words:

"We shall fight in France, we shall fight on the seas and oceans, we shall fight on the beaches, we shall fight on the landing grounds, We shall never surrender."

Quotes:

"Most of the important things in the world have been accomplished by people who have kept on trying when there seemed to be no hope at all."

— Dale Carnegie

"Hope is being able to see that there is light despite all of the darkness."

— Desmond Tutu

GRAND RISING DAY FIFTEEN

"When the world says, 'Give up,' hope whispers, 'Try it one more time.'"
— Unknown

"We must accept finite disappointment, but never lose infinite hope."
— Martin Luther King Jr.

"Hope is the thing with feathers that perches in the soul—and sings the tunes without the words—and never stops at all."
— Emily Dickinson

"Hope is a waking dream."
— Aristotle

"Everything that is done in this world is done by hope."
— Martin Luther

"Hope is the only thing stronger than fear."
— Suzanne Collins

"Keep your face always toward the sunshine—and shadows will fall behind you."
— Walt Whitman

"Once you choose hope, anything's possible."
— Christopher Reeve

"There is some good in this world, and it's worth fighting for."
— J.R.R. Tolkien

"All Faith. No Doubt!"
— Matthew C. Shaw

Bible Verses:

"May the God of hope fill you with all joy and peace as you trust in him, so that you may overflow with hope by the power of the Holy Spirit."
-Romans 15:13

"'For I know the plans I have for you,' declares the LORD, 'plans to prosper you and not to harm you, plans to give you hope and a future. Then you will call on me and come and pray to me, and I will listen to you. You will seek me and find me when you seek me with all your heart.'"
-Jeremiah 29:11-13

"We can rejoice, too, when we run into problems and trials, for we know that they help us develop endurance. And endurance develops strength of character, and character strengthens our confident hope of salvation. And this hope will not lead to disappointment. For we know how dearly God loves us, because he has given us the Holy Spirit to fill our hearts with his love."
-Romans 5:3-5 (NLT)

"So be strong and courageous, all you who put your hope in the Lord!"
-Psalm 31:24 (NLT)

"But those who trust in the Lord will find new strength. They will soar high on wings like eagles. They will run and not grow weary. They will walk and not faint."
-Isaiah 40:31 (NLT)

"The faithful love of the Lord never ends! His mercies never cease. Great is his faithfulness; his mercies begin afresh each morning. I say to myself, 'The Lord is my inheritance; therefore, I will hope in him!'"
-Lamentations 3:22-24 (NLT)

"Let us hold tightly without wavering to the hope we affirm, for God can be trusted to keep his promise."
-Hebrews 10:23 (NLT)

"Why am I discouraged? Why is my heart so sad? I will put my hope in God! I will praise him again—my Savior and my God!"
-Psalm 42:11 (NLT)

"All praise to God, the Father of our Lord Jesus Christ. It is by his great mercy that we have been born again, because God raised Jesus Christ from the dead. Now we live with great expectation."
-1 Peter 1:3 (NLT)

Today's Affirmations:

- I am filled with hope, even in the most challenging times.
- Hope gives me strength and courage to face any obstacle.
- I trust in the Lord's plans for my future, knowing they are for good and not for disaster.
- With hope in my heart, I rise above fear and uncertainty.
- Just as Winston Churchill inspired a nation, I inspire others through my unwavering resolve.
- I will fight for my goals and dreams, never surrendering to doubt or despair.
- Hope fills me with peace and confidence, empowering me to overcome any challenge.
- I walk with boldness and authority, knowing that victory is mine.
- Even in darkness, I keep my face toward the light, trusting in God's plan.
- With discipline and determination, I pursue my destiny with hope as my guide.

GRAND RISING DAY SIXTEEN

Don't Follow Your Heart or Your Flesh...
Follow God's Wisdom

The man who follows his heart is called a fool in the Bible, because the heart is not a source of wisdom, nor is it a reliable guide. Proverbs 28:26 (NLT) states, *"Those who trust their own insight are foolish, but anyone who walks in wisdom is safe."* This verse clearly warns against trusting our emotions or desires without godly wisdom.

You'll often hear people say, "Follow your heart," or "Do what you love." Yet, this advice can be dangerous. Many people who follow their heart or pursue only what they love find themselves in trouble. It's not always biblical to simply follow your passions. What if the things you love are wrong? What if they contradict God's Word? In such cases, we must not pursue them. I believe this is why so many people fall into sin—they follow their heart without considering God's will.

A strong example that I found to back up my convictions on this is the Biblical story of David... Although God called David a man after His own heart (1 Samuel 13:14), David made a tragic mistake when he followed his own desires. In 2 Samuel 11, David lusted after Bathsheba, the wife of Uriah. Rather than acting with integrity, he gave in to his sinful desires. David had an affair with Bathsheba, impregnated her, and then tried to cover up his sin.

When Uriah, a loyal soldier, refused to go home to his wife, David arranged for him to be killed on the battlefield.

The prophet Nathan later confronted David, revealing the gravity of his sin through a parable (2 Samuel 12). Although David repented and God forgave him, the consequences of his actions were severe.

Quotes:

"Your emotions are the slaves to your thoughts, and you are the slave to your emotions."

— Elizabeth Gilbert

"It is easier to suppress the first desire than to satisfy all that follow it."

— Benjamin Franklin

"Do not follow your inclination and natural desire, but always follow the road of duty."

— Immanuel Kant

"It is not reason that governs love."

— Molière

"What you want is often far less important than what you need."

— Unknown

"The first principle is that you must not fool yourself, and you are the easiest person to fool."

— Richard Feynman

"We can easily forgive a child who is afraid of the dark; the real tragedy of life is when men are afraid of the light."

— Plato

"The mind is its own place, and in itself can make a heaven of hell, a hell of heaven."

— John Milton

Bible Verses:

"Trust in the Lord with all your heart; do not depend on your own understanding. Seek his will in all you do, and he will show you which path to take."

-Proverbs 3:5-6 (NLT

"The human heart is the most deceitful of all things, and desperately wicked. Who really knows how bad it is?"

-Jeremiah 17:9 (NLT)

GRAND RISING DAY SIXTEEN

"Those who trust their own insight are foolish, but anyone who walks in wisdom is safe."
-Proverbs 28:26 (NLT)

"Your word is a lamp to guide my feet and a light for my path."
-Psalm 119:105 (NLT)

"But Jesus told him, 'No! The Scriptures say, 'People do not live by bread alone, but by every word that comes from the mouth of God.'"
-Matthew 4:4 (NLT)

"'My thoughts are nothing like your thoughts,' says the Lord. 'And my ways are far beyond anything you could imagine. For just as the heavens are higher than the earth, so my ways are higher than your ways and my thoughts higher than your thoughts.'"
-Isaiah 55:8-9 (NLT)

"We can make our plans, but the Lord determines our steps."
-Proverbs 16:9 (NLT)

"Take delight in the Lord, and he will give you your heart's desires. Commit everything you do to the Lord. Trust him, and he will help you."
-Psalm 37:4-5 (NLT)

Today's Affirmations:

- I trust in God's wisdom, not my own heart.
- I walk in wisdom, knowing that God directs my steps.
- I follow the Word of God as my guide and light.
- I seek God's will in all that I do, confident He will lead me on the right path.
- I choose integrity and reject desires that conflict with God's truth.
- I commit my heart and actions to God, trusting Him to align my desires with His purpose.
- I recognize that my emotions are not always reliable, but God's Word is.
- I lean on God's understanding, knowing His ways are higher than mine.
- I find strength and peace in knowing that God has plans for me, plans filled with hope and a future.
- I follow God's wisdom, knowing that it leads to safety and blessing.

with love,
Dad

GRAND RISING DAY SEVENTEEN

USING MONEY WITH INTEGRITY:
MONEY IS NOT THE ROOT OF ALL EVIL...
THE LOVE OF MONEY IS.

Money is often misunderstood. Many misquote the famous saying, "Money is the root of all evil." But the Bible clearly states in 1 Timothy 6:10, *"For the love of money is the root of all kinds of evil."* Money, in itself, is neutral—it's neither good nor evil. It is simply a tool that reflects the intentions of the person using it. Just as a hammer can be used to build a home or tear one down, money can be used to uplift or to destroy, depending on the heart of the person wielding it.

The truth is, money doesn't change a person—it reveals who they truly are. Someone with a heart for generosity and compassion will use their resources to give back, invest in others, and make the world a better place. You'll see them giving to those in need, supporting charitable causes, paying tithes, and offering alms to the less fortunate. Their wealth becomes a vessel for good, a way to reflect their values.

However, money can also expose selfishness, greed, and manipulation. Those who chase wealth for the sake of status or control often use it to manipulate others or indulge in their own desires, caring little for the consequences. They may exploit relationships, compromise their morals, or neglect the well-being of those around them—all for the sake of personal gain.

The problem isn't money; it's when we allow the love of money to control us. When we prioritize wealth above everything else, it can cloud our judgment and corrode our souls. In the pursuit of more—more success, more power, more material possessions—we often lose sight of what truly matters.

> *"The true richness of life doesn't come from material wealth; it comes from the connections we make, the love we share, and the impact we have on others."*

In a world that often equates success with financial wealth, it's easy to get caught up in the chase. But at what cost? While money can provide comfort and security, an excessive desire for it can lead to spiritual poverty. It can tempt us to put profits over people, to sacrifice relationships, and to compromise our values.

The true richness of life doesn't come from material wealth; it comes from the connections we make, the love we share, and the impact we have on others. Our worth isn't determined by how much money we have in the bank, but by the legacy we leave behind—the kindness we show, the lives we touch, the good we do.

When we choose people over profit, we remind ourselves that money is simply a tool, not the goal. It can be used to bless others, to create opportunities, to lift people up. But it should never be pursued at the expense of our humanity or our values. Money should work for us, not the other way around.

While it's important to manage our resources wisely and seek financial stability, we must never forget that money is not the essence of life. It's not the ultimate measure of success. No matter how much we accumulate, if we lack peace, purpose, and meaningful relationships, we are spiritually bankrupt.

Contentment comes not from how much we have but from understanding that what we do with our money is what truly counts. When we use it in alignment with our values, to serve others and honor God, it becomes a tool for good. When we prioritize love, kindness, and generosity, we create a legacy that far outlasts the fleeting nature of wealth.

Quotes:

"Is money good? Is money good? Many negative-minded persons say, "Money is the root of all evil." But the Bible says: Love of money is the root of all evil. And there is a big difference between the two even though one little word makes the difference."

— Napoleon Hill

Wealth consists not in having great possessions, but in having few wants."

— Epictetus

"Money often costs too much."

— Ralph Waldo Emerson

"It's not the man who has too little, but the man who craves more, that is poor."

— Seneca

"The real measure of your wealth is how much you'd be worth if you lost all your money."

— Anonymous

"Happiness is not in the mere possession of money; it lies in the joy of achievement, in the thrill of creative effort."

— Franklin D. Roosevelt

"We make a living by what we get, but we make a life by what we give."

— Winston Churchill

"Don't gain the world and lose your soul, wisdom is better than silver or gold."

— Bob Marley

Bible Verses:

"For the love of money is the root of all kinds of evil. And some people, craving money, have wandered from the true faith and pierced themselves with many sorrows."
-1 Timothy 6:10 (NLT)

"Good people leave an inheritance to their grandchildren, but the sinner's wealth passes to the godly."
-Proverbs 13:22 (NLT)

"No one can serve two masters. For you will hate one and love the other; you will be devoted to one and despise the other. You cannot serve God and be enslaved to money."
-Matthew 6:24 (NLT)

"Don't love money; be satisfied with what you have. For God has said, 'I will never fail you. I will never abandon you.'"

-Hebrews 13:5 (NLT)

"Those who love money will never have enough. How meaningless to think that wealth brings true happiness!"

-Ecclesiastes 5:10 (NLT)

"Then he said, 'Beware! Guard against every kind of greed. Life is not measured by how much you own.'"

-Luke 12:15 (NLT)

"Trust in your money and down you go! But the godly flourish like leaves in spring."

-Proverbs 11:28 (NLT)

"Don't store up treasures here on earth, where moths eat them and rust destroys them, and where thieves break in and steal. Store your treasures in heaven, where moths and rust cannot destroy, and thieves do not break in and steal. Wherever your treasure is, there the desires of your heart will also be."

-Matthew 6:19-21 (NLT)

"Choose a good reputation over great riches; being held in high esteem is better than silver or gold."

-Proverbs 22:1 (NLT)

"And I have been a constant example of how you can help those in need by working hard. You should remember the words of the Lord Jesus: 'It is more blessed to give than to receive.'"

-Acts 20:35 (NLT)

"Honor the Lord with your wealth and with the best part of everything you produce."

-Proverbs 3:9 (NLT)

Today's Affirmations:

- I choose people over profit, always prioritizing relationships over wealth.
- Money is a tool, and I use it wisely to create a positive impact.
- My value is not defined by my possessions but by my integrity and actions.
- I am content with what I have and grateful for life's true riches.
- I invest in others and give generously, knowing my wealth is measured in kindness and compassion.
- I control my money; it does not control me.
- I seek fulfillment through purpose and giving, not through material gain.
- I use my resources to uplift others and make the world a better place.
- I trust that my needs are met, and I am free from the love of money.
- I am wealthy in spirit, rich in relationships, and generous with my blessings.

with love,
Dad

GRAND RISING DAY EIGHTEEN

The Power of Perspective: Silver Lining Mentality
Window to The World: Cultivating a Positive Attitude

A person with a Negative Mental Attitude (NMA) might say, "I have to see it to believe it." This is a mindset of doubt, often referred to as a "Doubting Thomas" mentality. However, someone with a Positive Mental Attitude (PMA) says, "I know I'll see it, but first I have to believe it."

Your attitude is like the window through which you view the world. If your window is dirty or clouded with negativity, your outlook on life will be the same. George Bernard Shaw captured this idea when he famously said, "Better keep yourself clean and bright; you are the window through which you must see the world."

Having a PMA doesn't mean you're oblivious to the negative things in life. It's not about pretending there are no problems or burying your head in the sand. Instead, it's about maintaining the right expectations and believing that, despite challenges, you can overcome them.

I was hanging out with my mentor, Toby, while visiting his father, Gary. Toby asked his dad about some of the negative things that had happened and how he managed to handle them. Toby then told us, "My dad is one of the most positive people I've ever met." He looked so proud as he said this. Then, he asked rhetorically, "What would your dad have said?" That question hit me hard. I remembered my dad once telling me, with a sour face,

"Life is hard."

The difference in attitude was striking. Where my father saw hardship, Toby's father saw opportunity to overcome. That moment showed me how much our outlook shapes our reality. Positive outlooks lead to positive results.

<u>Quotes</u>:

"We just looked at things like it's no big deal. We have to handle them like we handle everything else in life and overcome."

— Gary Ayers

Attitude, not aptitude, determines altitude.

— John Maxwell

"A pessimist sees the difficulty in every opportunity; an optimist sees the opportunity in every difficulty."

— Winston Churchill:

"If you don't like something, change it. If you can't change it, change your attitude."

— Maya Angelou

"Whether you think you can, or you think you can't—you're right."

— Henry Ford:

"I never lose. I either win or learn."

— Nelson Mandela:

"The future belongs to those who believe in the beauty of their dreams."

— Eleanor Roosevelt

"Change your thoughts and you change your world."

— Norman Vincent Peale

"When we are no longer able to change a situation, we are challenged to change ourselves."

— Viktor Franklin

"Our greatest glory is not in never falling, but in rising every time we fall."

— Confucius

"The only person you are destined to become is the person you decide to be."

— Ralph Waldo Emerson

"Success is not the key to happiness. Happiness is the key to success. If you love what you are doing, you will be successful."

— Albert Schweitzer

Bible Verses:

"And now, dear brothers and sisters, one final thing. Fix your thoughts on what is true, and honorable, and right, and pure, and lovely, and admirable. Think about things that are excellent and worthy of praise."
–Philippians 4:8 (NLT)

"For as he thinks in his heart, so is he…"
–Proverbs 23:7 (NKJV)

"Don't copy the behavior and customs of this world, but let God transform you into a new person by changing the way you think. Then you will learn to know God's will for you, which is good and pleasing and perfect."
–Romans 12:2 (NLT)

"For we live by believing and not by seeing."
–2 Corinthians 5:7 (NLT)

"This is my command—be strong and courageous! Do not be afraid or discouraged. For the Lord your God is with you wherever you go."
–Joshua 1:9 (NLT)

"Don't be afraid, for I am with you. Don't be discouraged, for I am your God. I will strengthen you and help you. I will hold you up with my victorious right hand."
–Isaiah 41:10 (NLT)

"A glad heart makes a happy face; a broken heart crushes the spirit."
–Proverbs 15:13 (NLT)

"Think about the things of heaven, not the things of earth."
–Colossians 3:2 (NLT)

"Always be joyful. Never stop praying. Be thankful in all circumstances, for this is God's will for you who belong to Christ Jesus."
–1 Thessalonians 5:16-18 (NLT)

"You don't have enough faith," Jesus told them. "I tell you the truth, if you had faith even as small as a mustard seed, you could say to this mountain, 'Move from here to there,' and it would move. Nothing would be impossible."
–Matthew 17:20 (NLT)

Today's Affirmations:

- I choose to see the positive in every situation and embrace the opportunities that come my way.
- I have the power to transform my thoughts and shape my reality.
- I am resilient and capable of overcoming any challenge that arises.
- I believe in myself and my ability to create a fulfilling life.
- My attitude determines my direction, and I choose to focus on the good.
- I am grateful for the lessons that difficulties teach me, and I grow stronger from them.
- I see setbacks as stepping stones to success and growth.
- Every day, I cultivate a mindset of positivity, hope, and gratitude.
- I am worthy of happiness and success, and I attract positive experiences into my life.
- With every thought, I am planting seeds of positivity that will flourish in my life.
- I embrace change and welcome new opportunities with an open heart and mind.
- I trust in the process of life, knowing that everything is unfolding for my highest good.

with love,
Dad

GRAND RISING DAY NINETEEN

REREAD THIS!
DEVELOP A HEART OF GRATITUDE: ADOPT AN ATTITUDE OF GRATITUDE

Developing both a mindset and a heart set of gratitude will keep you from falling into the trap of envy and jealousy.vIn today's world, social media has amplified a spirit of comparison, often breeding jealousy and envy.

I can't tell you how many people I see online, posting about their "perfect" relationships, when in reality, I know their relationship is falling apart. They post about trips to Greece or Italy, not because everything is perfect, but because they are running from their problems. There's the real you, and then there's the social media version of you. Stop comparing yourself to others and follow Jesus!

Set aside time every day to give thanks to God. Reflect on where you've been and how God has brought you through. Sometimes, you need to stop and consider just how far you've come. Someone once told me, "If you don't think you were a fool when you were younger, you probably still are." (lol) But as you look back, thank God for the experiences that matured you and provided you with wisdom.

Six Ways to Develop a Heart and Attitude of Gratitude:[7]

1. Set aside time every day to thank God - Cultivate a daily habit of gratitude.
2. Trust that what God has for you is yours - Stop striving for what others have.
3. Stop comparing yourself to others - Focus on your own journey.
4. Find peace in your current season - Understand that each season has a purpose.
5. Celebrate others' successes - Rejoice with others without envy.
6. Spend time with God - Let God's presence shape your perspective.

Quotes:

"Gratitude turns what we have into enough."

— Aesop

"Comparison is the thief of joy."

— Theodore Roosevelt

"Don't compare your chapter 1 to someone else's chapter 20."

— Unknown

"The only person you should try to be better than is the person you were yesterday."

— Matty Mullins

"To be yourself in a world that is constantly trying to make you something else is the greatest accomplishment."

— Ralph Waldo Emerson

"A grateful heart is a magnet for miracles."

— Unknown

"Success is not how high you have climbed, but how you make a positive difference to the world."

— Roy T. Bennett

"The more you praise and celebrate your life, the more there is in life to celebrate."

— Oprah Winfrey

Bible Verses:

"Be thankful in all circumstances, for this is God's will for you who belong to Christ Jesus.
-1 Thessalonians 5:18 (NLT)

"Let us not become conceited, or provoke one another, or be jealous of one another."
-Galatians 5:26 (NLT)

"Pay careful attention to your own work, for then you will get the satisfaction of a job well done, and you won't need to compare yourself to anyone else."
-Galatians 6:4 (NLT)

"Humble yourselves before the Lord, and he will lift you up in honor."
-James 4:10 (NLT)

"I know how to live on almost nothing or with everything. I have learned the secret of living in every situation, whether it is with a full stomach or empty, with plenty or little."
-Philippians 4:12 (NLT)

"Don't worry about anything; instead, pray about everything. Tell God what you need, and thank him for all he has done."
-Philippians 4:6 (NLT)

"Be happy with those who are happy, and weep with those who weep."
-Romans 12:15 (NLT)

"I press on to reach the end of the race and receive the heavenly prize for which God, through Christ Jesus, is calling us."
-Philippians 3:14 (NLT)

Today's Affirmations:

- I am grateful for where God has brought me, and I trust His plan for my life
- I release envy and jealousy, knowing that what God has for me is mine.
- I stop comparing myself to others and focus on my own journey with Jesus.
- I find peace and comfort in the season I'm in, trusting God's timing.
- I celebrate the success of others, knowing that my blessings are on the way
- I dedicate time each day to thank God for His faithfulness and guidance.
- Spending time with God shapes my heart and perspective, helping me see life through His eyes.
- I reflect on how far I've come and thank God for the wisdom gained through every experience.

with love,
Dad

GRAND RISING DAY TWENTY

FIND A MENTOR
"YOU ARE LIMITED TO THE KNOWLEDGE IN YOUR OWN MIND."

I found mentorship unintentionally—I simply fell into it. But it has blessed me more than I could have ever imagined. I wasn't actively seeking it, but I'm forever grateful that I found it because it changed the entire trajectory of my life for the better.

Financially, I used to be a big spender, but through mentorship, I learned how to tithe, save, invest, and diversify. Spiritually, my walk with God is stronger, and I'm now leading ministries at my church. My relationships have also flourished, especially my marriage, as I've learned how to communicate and compromise.

Looking back as both a protégé and mentor, I encourage others to seek mentorship in three key areas: Financial, Spiritual, and Relational. This could come from the same person or different people. Sometimes, a relational mentor may be a counselor or someone who has had a successful marriage for many years. If you're married, finding a good marriage counselor can make a huge difference. Just remember, not all counselors are created equal—do your research to find the right one.

The best advice regarding mentors and protégés that I have come across have come from the book "The Pursuit; Success is hidden in the Journey"[8] by Dexter Yager. In regards to mentors he says:

Pick your mentors and pick them well. Look at the ones that have had long term success. There's a big difference between long term success and something that's a mess. You've got to have goals, and you need somebody to help stretch your goals.

Mentors are trusted teachers. Various teachers will enter and exit your life. The Holy Spirit is your dominant and most important Mentor of all. (See Jn. 14:15,16)

Wisdom Determines the success of your life. There are two ways to receive wisdom: Mistakes and Mentors. Mentors are the difference between poverty and prosperity; decrease and increase; loss and gain; pain and pleasure; deterioration and restoration.

1. An uncommon mentor is the master key to the success of a protégé. Wisdom is the principal thing. (Prov. 4:7)
2. An uncommon mentor Transfers wisdom through relationship. He that walketh with wise men shall be wise; but a companion of fools shall be destroyed. (Prov. 13:20)
3. An uncommon mentor guarantees your promotion.
4. An uncommon mentor can determine your wealth.
5. An uncommon mentor can paralyze your enemies against you.
6. An uncommon mentor can influence people to listen to you.
7. An uncommon mentor will require your pursuit. He does not need what you know. You need what he knows.
8. An uncommon mentor is more interested in your success than your affection. His focus is not the celebration of you, but the correction of you.
9. An uncommon mentor is not necessarily your best friend:
    - Your best friend loves you the way you are. Your mentor loves you too much to leave you the way you are.
    - Your best friend is comfortable with your past. Your mentor is comfortable with your future.
    - Your best friend ignores your weakness. A mentor removes your weakness.
    - Your best friend is your cheerleader. A mentor is your coach.
    - Your best friend sees what you do right. Your mentor sees what you do wrong.
10. A mentor sees things that you cannot see. He sees weaknesses in you before you experience the pain of them. He sees an enemy before you dis-

cern him. He has already experienced the pain of a problem you are about to create.
11. An uncommon mentor will become an enemy to the enemies of his protégé.
12. An Uncommon Mentor can create an Uncommon Protege. Everything you know will come through Mentorship, by experience or a person. Invest everything to spend time and moments with an Uncommon Mentor God has chosen to sow into your life.

In regards to protégés he says:
"A protégé' is an obedient learner."

The wisdom of a mentor is perpetuated through a protégé. True success will produce a successor. Jesus took 12 protégés and revolutionized the Earth. It is very important that you recognize those connected to you by the Holy Spirit for the multiplying and perpetuation of your success and life.

You will only remember what you teach another. Our children should become our protégés. Passive Protégés only reach when it is convenient, or when their personal efforts do not produce their desired result. They subconsciously expect their mentor to produce success for them.

Parasite Protégés pursue for credibility, not correction. They will use the name and influence of a mentor to manipulate others into a relationship. They want what the mentor has earned, not what he has learned. They want a reputation without preparation.

Prodigal Protégés enter and exit the relationship freely. When serious correction occurs, they move toward another mentor who has not yet discovered their flaws. They distance themselves when their mentor encounters personal difficulties, loss of credibility, or false accusation or persecution. They only return when their pigpen becomes unbearable.

Productive Protégés are uncommon. They have a servant's heart. They never make a major decision without the council and feedback of their mentor. They view their mentor as a dominant gift from God. They love their mentor as much as themselves.

The uncommon protégé assigned by God will honor the mentor. And we beseech you, brother, to know them which labor among you, and over you in the Lord, and admonish you; and to esteem them very highly in love for their works sake," (1Thess. 5:12,13).

LEGACY OF WISDOM

1. The uncommon protégé will invest everything to stay in the presence of the uncommon mentor.
2. The uncommon protégé follows the council from the uncommon mentor.
3. The uncommon protégé reveals the secrets and dreams of his heart with the mento. Vulnerability Creates the unbreakable bond between a mentor and the protégé.
4. The uncommon protégé freely discusses his mistakes and pain with the mentor.
5. The uncommon protégé defines clearly his expectations to the mentor.
6. The uncommon protégé gladly sows seeds of appreciation back into the life of the mentor.
7. The uncommon protégé ultimately receives the mantle of the mentor he serves.
8. The uncommon protégé moves toward the shelter of the mentor during a season of uncommon attack and warfare.
9. The uncommon protégé will change his own schedule to invest time in the presence of the mentor.
10. The uncommon protégé is someone who discerns, respects, and pursues the answers God has stored in the mentor for his or her life.

Quotes:

"Learn from people that are walking down the mountain that you are ready to climb."

— Toby Ayers

If I have seen farther than others, it is because I have stood on the shoulders of giants.

— Sir Issac Newton

"Don't be like us... be like minded..."

— Toby Ayers

"So many people are jealous of your success, but no one is jealous of what you had to go through to get it."

— Unknown (Toby Ayers)

"The only true wisdom is in knowing you know nothing."

— Socrates

"A mentor is someone who allows you to see the hope inside yourself."
— Oprah Winfrey

"Criticism, like rain, should be gentle enough to nourish a man's growth without destroying his roots."
— Frank A. Clark

"We all need people who will give us feedback. That's how we improve."
— Bill Gates

"The delicate balance of mentoring someone is not creating them in your own image, but giving them the opportunity to create themselves."
— Steven Spielberg

"If you cannot see where you are going, ask someone who has been there before."
— J. Loren Norris

"The more you know yourself, the more clarity there is. Self-knowledge has no end—you don't come to an achievement; you don't come to a conclusion. It is an endless river."
— Jiddu Krishnamurti

"Your own self-realization is the greatest service you can render the world."
— Ramana Maharshi

"Wealth consists not in having great possessions, but in having few wants."
— Epictetus

"Do not save what is left after spending; instead, spend what is left after saving."
— Warren Buffett

"The single biggest problem in communication is the illusion that it has taken place."
— George Bernard Shaw

"In a conflict, being willing to change allows you to move from a point of view to a viewing point—a higher, more expansive place, from which you can see both sides."
— Thomas Crum

"Success is not the key to happiness. Happiness is the key to success. If you love what you are doing, you will be successful."
— Albert Schweitzer

"Success is not how high you have climbed, but how you make a positive difference to the world."

— Roy T. Bennett

Bible Verses:

"Walk with the wise and become wise; associate with fools and get in trouble."
-Proverbs 13:20

"Getting wisdom is the wisest thing you can do! And whatever else you do, develop good judgment."
-Proverbs 4:7

"To learn, you must love discipline; it is stupid to hate correction."
-Proverbs 12:1

"No discipline is enjoyable while it is happening—it's painful! But afterward there will be a peaceful harvest of right living for those who are trained in this way."
-Hebrews 12:11

"Get all the advice and instruction you can, so you will be wise the rest of your life."
-Proverbs 19:20

"Plans go wrong for lack of advice; many advisers bring success."
-Proverbs 15:22

"But when the Father sends the Advocate as my representative—that is, the Holy Spirit—he will teach you everything and will remind you of everything I have told you."
-John 14:26

"And you should imitate me, just as I imitate Christ."
-1 Corinthians 11:1

"You have heard me teach things that have been confirmed by many reliable witnesses. Now teach these truths to other trustworthy people who will be able to pass them on to others."
-2 Timothy 2:2

"Keep putting into practice all you learned and received from me—everything you heard from me and saw me doing. Then the God of peace will be with you."
-Philippians 4:9

"Dear friend, I hope all is well with you and that you are as healthy in body as you are strong in spirit."
-3 John 1:2

"Study this Book of Instruction continually. Meditate on it day and night so you will be sure to obey everything written in it. Only then will you prosper and succeed in all you do."
-Joshua 1:8

Today's Affirmations:

- I welcome mentorship into my life, knowing it can change my trajectory for the better.
- I am committed to growing financially, spiritually, and relationally through the wisdom of others.
- I embrace financial wisdom—I tithe, save, invest, and diversify with purpose.
- My walk with God strengthens daily, and I am guided to lead and serve in meaningful ways.
- My relationships thrive as I learn to communicate, compromise, and nurture them.
- I seek mentorship in areas where I need growth, knowing that wise counsel elevates my life.
- I am intentional in finding mentors with long-term success who can stretch my goals and vision.
- I pursue wisdom through trusted mentors and understand that their correction is essential for my growth.
- I honor the mentors in my life and am open to learning from their experiences.
- I invest time and energy in the mentors God has placed in my life, knowing they hold valuable keys to my success.
- I am a faithful protégé, receptive to guidance and grateful for the wisdom shared with me.
- I discern and appreciate the God-given connections in my life that will help me multiply and perpetuate success.

with love,
Dad

GRAND RISING DAY TWENTY-ONE

Unlock Your Potential
You Have Potential—Now it's Time to Turn That Potential into Something Great!

There's a significant difference between potential energy and kinetic energy. According to Merriam-Webster, **potential energy** is "existing in possibility, capable of development into actuality." It's the stored energy in an object due to its position, properties, or forces acting on it, such as gravitational, elastic, magnetic, or electric energy. Simply put, potential energy is energy waiting to be activated.

But here's the reality: Potential means you could be great, but until you take action, it remains untapped. In my words: "You could be awesome in the future, but you suck right now." To transform that potential into something real, you need kinetic energy —the energy of motion. Kinetic energy means action. You have to move, do, and create.

For years, I had the potential to write a book, but I procrastinated. Eventually, I made a decision, took action, and transformed that potential into reality—this book you're reading now is the result of that kinetic energy.

Years ago, I had a conversation with my wife's nephew about his future. He was unsure of his path, and I bluntly told him, "You don't want a life that sucks." It wasn't the most elegant advice, but it left an impression. To this day, he remembers those words and how they pushed him to take initiative.

> Yes sir a life that doesn't suck haha
>
> This Thursday
>
> You remember that quote huh??
>
> That's a good quote to have
>
> You remember the exact quote?
>
> Not exactly haha
>
> I think you said "You don't want a life that sucks" haha

Take action today—don't wait. Start that business, finish that degree, get that gym membership and begin your fitness journey. Start saving your money, build an emergency fund, save for that house, write that book, or even read the Bible from cover to cover.

- Prepare for success before you need it—dig your well before you're thirsty.
- Take action, prepare for success, and trust in God's strength as you pursue your potential.

To unlock your potential, you must first overcome doubt and take action. Waiting for the perfect moment only delays progress. Success is built through consistent effort, not idle hesitation.

Like kinetic energy, potential remains dormant until it's transformed into action. Until you take that first step, your capabilities are untapped. This mirrors the concept of preparing in advance—"digging your well before you're thirsty." Taking action now positions you for future success, just as preparing ahead ensures you're ready when opportunities arise.

Consistent effort, much like continuous motion, leads to progress. It's about moving from potential to action, making plans, and acting on them immediately. This combination of preparation and motion propels you toward a strong future.

God has equipped you with the ability to be bold and disciplined. He has plans for you, but those plans only come to life when you take action and walk in faith. Don't wait for the perfect moment. Act now to unlock your potential. Action cures fear! Success is not accidental; it's the product of preparation, wisdom, and bold, disciplined action. With a foundation of preparation and wisdom, you create lasting success and align yourself with God's purpose.

Quotes:

"When you avoid failure you also avoid success."
— Robert Kyosaki

"The only limit to our realization of tomorrow is our doubts of today."
— Franklin D. Roosevelt

"Success usually comes to those who are too busy to be looking for it."
— Henry David Thoreau

"The way to get started is to quit talking and begin doing."
— Walt Disney

"You don't have to be great to start, but you have to start to be great."
— Zig Ziglar

"The best time to plant a tree was 20 years ago. The second best time is now."
— Chinese Proverb

"What you do today can improve all your tomorrows."
— Ralph Marston

"Don't watch the clock; do what it does. Keep going."
— Sam Levenson

"Action is the foundational key to all success."
— Pablo Picasso

"The future depends on what you do today."
— Mahatma Gandhi

"Dream big. Start small. Act now."
— Robin Sharma

Bible Verses:

For I can do everything through Christ, who gives me strength.
-Philippians 4:13

So you see, faith by itself isn't enough. Unless it produces good deeds, it is dead and useless.
-James 2:17

Lazy people want much but get little, but those who work hard will prosper.
-Proverbs 13:4

"Farmers who wait for perfect weather never plant. If they watch every cloud, they never harvest."
-Ecclesiastes 11:4

"For God has not given us a spirit of fear and timidity, but of power, love, and self-discipline."
-2 Timothy 1:7

"Good planning and hard work lead to prosperity, but hasty shortcuts lead to poverty."
-Proverbs 21:5

"Work willingly at whatever you do, as though you were working for the Lord rather than for people."
-Colossians 3:23

"Do your planning and prepare your fields before building your house."
-Proverbs 24:27

"For I know the plans I have for you," says the Lord. "They are plans for good and not for disaster, to give you a future and a hope."
-Jeremiah 29:11

"Anyone who listens to my teaching and follows it is wise, like a person who builds a house on solid rock. Though the rain comes in torrents and the floodwaters rise and the winds beat against that house, it won't collapse because it is built on bedrock."
-Matthew 7:24-25

Today's Affirmations:

- I have untapped potential, and today, I choose to turn it into greatness.
- I am capable of transforming possibility into reality through action.
- I will no longer let my potential remain dormant; I take steps to activate it.
- I am driven by kinetic energy—I take action, move forward, and create change.
- I will not procrastinate on my dreams; I will take decisive steps to achieve them.
- I take responsibility for my future and prepare for success before I need it.
- I have the power to build the life I want through consistent effort and action.
- I embrace challenges as opportunities to turn potential energy into progress.
- My actions today will shape the greatness I achieve tomorrow.
- I am prepared for the future because I dig my well before I am thirsty.

GRAND RISING
DAY TWENTY-TWO

What To Do When Things Are Not Going Your Way...

Life doesn't always unfold the way we expect. Sometimes, it feels like no matter what we do, things keep falling apart. I've experienced that firsthand. When both my parents fell ill, I stepped in to take care of them. Two years after they passed, my oldest brother suffered a stroke. These moments were crushing, and yet they also brought me to a critical decision: when things aren't going your way, what will you do?

The world says to complain, feel sorry for yourself, or look for someone to blame. But the Bible calls us to respond differently. As believers, we are called to praise the Lord, even when life takes unexpected turns. Here's what I've learned through my own trials and from powerful sermons, including one by Jamie Jones:

1. Stay Faithful to God

Our faithfulness to God isn't tied to whether we get what we want or if life goes smoothly. Faithfulness means standing firm even when life doesn't seem fair. Your integrity—your actions and responses—must come from a deep-rooted desire to serve and honor God, not for any earthly reward. We remain faithful because God is faithful.

"Consider it pure joy, my brothers and sisters, whenever you face trials of many kinds, be-

cause you know that the testing of your faith produces perseverance."

— James 1:2-3

2. Stay Focused and Keep Pushing Ahead

It's tempting to give up when things go wrong. But success in God's plan comes from staying the course. No matter how hard things get, stay focused on your purpose. God doesn't abandon His children in times of difficulty, and He rewards persistence.

3. Don't Be a Crybaby

This might sound harsh, but it's a needed reminder. Self-pity doesn't bring solutions. It only keeps you stuck in the same place. God calls us to rise above the temptation to complain and instead rely on His strength. You may have moments of vulnerability—after all, we are human—but don't let those moments define your response.

4. You Will Be Rewarded in Due Season

God promises that there is a reward for those who endure. Your hard work, your sacrifices, your commitment to righteousness will not go unnoticed by Him. Sometimes it feels like the harvest will never come, but as Galatians 6:9 says, *"Let us not become weary in doing good, for at the proper time we will reap a harvest if we do not give up."* The key is to keep going even when you don't see the fruit immediately.

5. Place Your Trust in the Lord

When life feels out of control, we have to place our trust in the only One who is always in control—God. You might not understand why certain things are happening, but you can trust that God knows what He is doing. Romans 8:28 reassures us that "all things work together for good for those who love God and are called according to His purpose."

> *"God doesn't abandon His children in times of difficulty, and He rewards persistence."*

Everything may not make sense now, but God is working behind the scenes. He knows the end from the beginning, and He is weaving all the pieces of your life together for His glory.

In the most difficult seasons of life, God is still at work. He sees the big picture even when we can only see a small part. And what He is crafting is always for your ultimate good, even if it doesn't feel like it in the moment. Hold on to that truth.

I like to think of life as a camera. Ziad K. Abdelnour once said, "Life is like a camera. Focus on what's important. Capture the good times. And if things don't work out, just take another shot." We have to stay focused on what's eternal—our relationship with God, the love we give, and the purpose we pursue. Even when things go wrong, God offers us the chance to take another shot, to learn, to grow, and to move forward.

In your darkest moments, praise the Lord. Keep your integrity, keep pushing ahead, and trust that His plan for your life is unfolding—even when things don't seem to go your way. God is faithful, and you will be rewarded in due season. Keep believing, keep moving, and keep praising.

Quotes:

"Life is like a camera. Focus on what's important. Capture the good times. And if things don't work out, just take another shot."
— Ziad K. Abdelnour

"Integrity is doing the right thing, even when no one is watching."
— C.S. Lewis

"Success is not the key to happiness. Happiness is the key to success. If you love what you are doing, you will be successful."
— Albert Schweitzer

"It does not matter how slowly you go as long as you do not stop."
— Confucius

"Fall seven times, stand up eight."
— Japanese Proverb

"Our greatest glory is not in never falling, but in rising every time we fall."
— Confucius

"Life is 10% what happens to us and 90% how we react to it."
— Charles R. Swindoll

"Difficulties in life are intended to make us better, not bitter."
— Dan Reeves

"Tough times never last, but tough people do."
— Robert H. Schuller

"The best way out is always through."
— Robert Frost

"All things are difficult before they are easy."
— Thomas Fuller

Bible Verses:

"To do what is right and just is more acceptable to the Lord than sacrifice."
-Proverbs 21:3 (NLT)

"Whatever you do, work at it with all your heart, as working for the Lord, not for human masters."
-Colossians 3:23 (NLT)

"Forgetting what is behind and straining toward what is ahead, I press on toward the goal to win the prize for which God has called me heavenward in Christ Jesus."
-Philippians 3:13-14 (NLT)

"But those who hope in the Lord will renew their strength. They will soar on wings like eagles; they will run and not grow weary, they will walk and not be faint."
-Isaiah 40:31 (NLT)

"Blessed is the one who perseveres under trial because, having stood the test, that person will receive the crown of life that the Lord has promised to those who love him."
-James 1:12 (NLT)

"Be joyful in hope, patient in affliction, faithful in prayer."
-Romans 12:12 (NLT)

"I will bless the Lord at all times; His praise shall continually be in my mouth."
-Psalm 34:1 (NLT)

"And we know that in all things God works for the good of those who love him, who have been called according to his purpose."
-Romans 8:28 (NLT)

"For I know the plans I have for you, declares the Lord, plans to prosper you and not to harm you, plans to give you hope and a future."
-Jeremiah 29:11 (NLT)

Today's Affirmations:

- I act with integrity, knowing my faithfulness is seen by God, even when the rewards are not immediate.
- I work with all my heart, as if working for the Lord, and trust that my efforts are valuable.
- I press on, no matter how slow the journey, knowing that persistence will bring the reward in due season.
- When I fall, I rise again, stronger and more determined, trusting that God is renewing my strength.
- I embrace challenges as opportunities for growth and trust that God's

plan for me is good.
- I choose joy, patience, and hope, knowing that God is working behind the scenes for my good.
- I will bless the Lord at all times, maintaining a heart of praise, even in adversity.
- I trust that God is working all things together for my good, even when I cannot see the outcome.
- I believe that God has plans to prosper me and give me hope, and I walk confidently in His purpose for my life.
- I rest in the knowledge that God's timing is perfect, and I will receive my reward in due season.

with love,
Dad

GRAND RISING DAY TWENTY-THREE

Embrace Your Inner Warrior: Drawing Strength from God, the Ultimate Warrior

The powerful truth is that God is not only our Creator and Savior, but also our greatest Warrior. *"The Lord is a warrior; Yahweh is his name!"* Exodus 15:3 (NLT) The Bible is filled with examples of God fighting for His people, leading them into battle, and securing victory on their behalf. And just as God is a warrior, He has equipped each of us with the strength, courage, and ability to fight our own battles. You are a warrior, created in His image, empowered to stand firm, and overcome any obstacle.

You may not always feel like a warrior, but that doesn't change the truth. God has called you to be strong and courageous, to face the challenges of life with boldness, and to trust in His strength. The story of Elisha in 2 Kings 6:16-17 shows us that there is more going on than we can see with our natural eyes. God's armies are greater than any force that comes against us. *"Do not fear, for those who are with us are more than those who are with them"*—this is the confidence we can have as warriors of God.

As Martin Luther King Jr. once said, "Courage faces fear and thereby masters it." This is the essence of a warrior—standing strong in the face of fear, trusting in God to fight alongside you. You cannot allow fear or uncertainty to paralyze you. Instead, you must move forward, even when the path ahead seems unclear. This courage is not born from your own strength but from God's power working in and through you.

If you haven't seen anyone around you stand up and fight for what's right, you must be the one to stand. Warriors don't wait for someone else to lead the charge—they rise up and act, trusting in God's provision. God has equipped us with the ability to take action, to be bold, and to be disciplined. He has plans for us, but those plans come to life only when we take steps of faith.

Jesus is the ultimate warrior. He is called the Lion of Judah, and He has triumphed over every enemy—sin, death, fear, and the Devil himself. Revelation 5:5 reminds us, *"Do not weep! See, the Lion of the tribe of Judah... has triumphed."* Just as Jesus conquered all, we too are called to live in victory, empowered by His Spirit.

Throughout the Bible, God continually tells His people to be strong and courageous. From Joshua's call to lead the Israelites into the Promised Land (Joshua 1:9) to David's words to Solomon (1 Chronicles 28:20), the message is clear: courage is essential in fulfilling God's purpose for our lives. But this courage isn't something we muster up on our own—it comes from knowing that God is with us, that He will never leave us, and that He has already gone ahead of us.

The Lord reveals Himself in power and compassion in Exodus 34:5-8: "The Lord! The God of compassion and mercy! I am slow to anger and filled with unfailing love and faithfulness." God is both mighty and merciful, fighting for us as our Warrior, but also guiding us with love and patience.

The "Lord of Armies" is with us—a military term that signifies God as our Warrior, fighting on our behalf. He is the strongest of all, the One who never retreats, never fails. As the Lion of Judah, Jesus has triumphed over every force that stands against us.

The Hebrew war cry "RAK CHAZAK" embodies this warrior mentality—it means to do nothing but be strong and courageous! It's a reminder that no matter what you face, God is with you as your Warrior God. He fights for you, and He calls you to stand firm, to be unshakable in your trust in Him.

In the end, being a warrior for God means trusting Him in every battle, knowing that He is with you, and standing firm in the face of adversity. You are not just fighting your battles alone—God, the ultimate Warrior, is fighting for you. Stand up, take action, and embrace the warrior spirit within you!

To close, I want to share an excerpt from one of my favorite songs. It perfectly aligns with the message of this chapter, reminding us of God's power and the call to rise up as warriors in faith.

"Lion" (Excerpt)
Song by Elevation Worship

God of Jacob, Great I Am
King of angels, Son of Man
Voice of many waters
Song of Heaven's throne
Louder than the thunder
Make Your glory known

Hail, hail Lion of Judah
Let the Lion roar
Hail, hail Lion of Judah
Let the Lion roar
Roar! (Roar!)
Roar! (Roar!)

Prepare the way
Prepare the way of the Lord
O valley, be raised up
O mountain, be made low
Roar! (Roar!)
Let the Lion roar!

Quotes:

"Courage is not the absence of fear, but rather the judgment that something else is more important than fear."

— Ambrose Redmoon

"He who is not courageous enough to take risks will accomplish nothing in life."

— Muhammad Ali

"You gain strength, courage, and confidence by every experience in which you really stop to look fear in the face."

— Eleanor Roosevelt

"The way to get started is to quit talking and begin doing."

— Walt Disney

"Do not wait; the time will never be 'just right.' Start where you stand, and work with whatever tools you may have at your command."

— George Herbert

"Inaction breeds doubt and fear. Action breeds confidence and courage. If you want to conquer fear, do not sit home and think about it. Go out and get busy."

— Dale Carnegie

"Success is where preparation and opportunity meet."

— Bobby Unser

"By failing to prepare, you are preparing to fail."

— Benjamin Franklin

"Give me six hours to chop down a tree and I will spend the first four sharpening the axe."

— Abraham Lincoln

"Strength does not come from physical capacity. It comes from an indomitable will."

— Mahatma Gandhi

"The only limit to our realization of tomorrow will be our doubts of today."

— Franklin D. Roosevelt

"Success is not final, failure is not fatal: It is the courage to continue that counts."

— Winston Churchill

Bible Verses:

"So be strong and courageous! Do not be afraid and do not panic before them. For the Lord your God will personally go ahead of you. He will neither fail you nor abandon you."
-Deuteronomy 31:6 (NLT)

"This is my command—be strong and courageous! Do not be afraid or discouraged. For the Lord your God is with you wherever you go."
-Joshua 1:9 (NLT)

"Then one of the elders said to me, "Do not weep! See, the Lion of the tribe of Judah, the Root of David, has triumphed. He is able to open the scroll and its seven seals."
-Revelation 5:5 (NLT)

"The Lord will march out like a mighty man, like a warrior He will stir up His zeal."
-Isaiah 42:13 (NLT)

"...Do not be afraid, for those who are with us are more than those who are with them."
-2 Kings 6:16-17 (AMP)

"Don't be afraid, for I am with you. Don't be discouraged, for I am your God. I will strengthen you and help you. I will hold you up with my victorious right hand."
-Isaiah 41:10 (NLT)

"But don't just listen to God's word. You must do what it says. Otherwise, you are only fooling yourselves."
-James 1:22 (NLT)

"Commit your actions to the Lord, and your plans will succeed."
-Proverbs 16:3 (NLT)

"Farmers who wait for perfect weather never plant. If they watch every cloud, they never harvest."
-Ecclesiastes 11:4 (NLT)

"The horse is prepared for the day of battle, but the victory belongs to the Lord."
-Proverbs 21:31 (NASB)

"For I can do everything through Christ, who gives me strength."
-Philippians 4:13 (NLT)

Today's Affirmations:

- I am strong and courageous because God is with me wherever I go.
- I am a warrior, and I fight with God's strength, not my own.
- I will not fear because the Lord of Armies is fighting for me.
- I walk in the victory that Jesus has already won.
- I rise up in boldness, knowing that God has equipped me for battle.
- I fear nothing because God strengthens me, upholds me, and fights for me.
- I am bold and confident, knowing that victory rests in the hands of the Lord.
- I stand firm in the face of fear because my God is a mighty warrior who fights for me.
- I will not wait for the perfect moment—I act now, trusting that God will guide my steps.
- I take bold, decisive action, knowing that success is built through consistent effort.
- I overcome doubt by stepping out in faith, knowing that God equips me for success.
- I am prepared for the future because I trust in God's wisdom and provision.
- I take action today, knowing that preparation leads to success, and God is my provider.
- I plan with wisdom and act in faith, knowing that God is my refuge and strength.
- Through Christ, I have already triumphed over fear, doubt, and obstacles.
- I am victorious through Christ, who strengthens me to overcome every challenge.
- I am more than a conqueror because God fights for me and goes before me.
- The Lord is with me in every battle, and He will never leave me or forsake me.
- I walk confidently, knowing that God goes before me, preparing the way for victory.
- I am protected by the Lord of Armies, who leads me into victory over every challenge.

GRAND RISING
DAY TWENTY-FOUR

The Power of Reading and Studying The Bible

Reading the Bible is more than just a daily task; it's a life-giving habit that shapes our hearts, minds, and souls. Proverbs, in particular, is a powerful book to study, offering timeless wisdom for daily living. But the transformative power of the Bible goes beyond simply knowing the words on the page—it's in the way God uses those words to speak directly to us in different seasons of our lives.

As C.S. Lewis once said, "Read many books but live in the Bible." Books can teach us much about life, success, and the world around us, but only the Bible gives us the wisdom to live in alignment with God's will. When we anchor ourselves in Scripture, we are not just gaining knowledge; we are preparing our hearts to receive divine guidance.

One of the most remarkable things about the Bible is that you can read the same Scripture multiple times, and each time it will speak to you in a different way. Jentezen Franklin beautifully captures this truth, likening it to the Greek philosopher Heraclitus's saying, "You never step into the same river twice." In the same way, you never read the same Bible verse the same way twice.

This is because the Bible isn't just words on a page. It's divinely inspired and living. God, the heavenly Author, knows everything about you—

your circumstances, desires, fears, past, and future. He knows what you need in each moment of your life. That's why the same verse can comfort you in one season, challenge you in another, and convict you in yet another. The difference is how God illuminates those words in light of what you're going through. But to experience this, you must make time to read and meditate on the Word.

Cultivating Sensitivity to God's Voice

As we set our minds on things above, as Colossians 3:2 encourages, we need to cultivate our sensitivity to God's voice. This requires more than just reading—it requires studying and meditating on Scripture. The more we familiarize ourselves with the Bible, the more attuned we become to the Holy Spirit's guidance.

You may read a verse today, and it may not stand out to you. But in a week, a month, or a year, God might bring that same verse to your mind with new meaning and clarity. The Bible isn't static because God isn't static. He is always working in us and around us, shaping us for His purposes.

Practical Steps for Engaging with Scripture

- Set aside daily time to read the Bible, even if it's just a few verses. The more consistent you are, the more opportunities you give God to speak to you.
- Pray before you read, asking God to reveal what He wants you to see in the passage.
- Meditate on key verses throughout the day. When a verse resonates with you, write it down, and think on it. Let it guide your thoughts and actions.
- Be patient and open. Some days, a passage may not feel impactful, but trust that God will use His Word in your life at the right time.
- Study Proverbs regularly. Proverbs is filled with practical wisdom, and its teachings are timeless and always relevant, no matter what stage of life you're in.

We live in a world full of distractions, but the Bible gives us the grounding we need to navigate life with clarity and purpose. Let the Bible be your guide, your foundation, and your source of wisdom. As C.S. Lewis said, "Read many books but live in the Bible." Keep your heart and mind fixed on heavenly things, and trust that God will meet you in His Word.

When you immerse yourself in Scripture, you're not just learning about God—you're encountering Him in real time, allowing Him to shape your life according to His perfect will.

<u>Quotes</u>:

"Read many books but live in the Bible."
— CS Lewis

"A room without books is like a body without a soul."
— Cicero

"Reading is to the mind what exercise is to the body."
— Joseph Addison

"The more that you read, the more things you will know. The more that you learn, the more places you'll go."
— Dr. Seuss

"We don't see things as they are, we see them as we are."
— Anaïs Nin

"The only true wisdom is in knowing you know nothing."
— Socrates

"The more I read, the more I acquire, the more certain I am that I know nothing."
— Voltaire

"Each time you love, love as deeply as if it were forever - only, nothing is eternal."
— Audre Lorde

"It is not what you look at that matters, it's what you see."
— Henry David Thoreau

"The only thing that is constant is change."
— Heraclitus

"Change is the law of life. And those who look only to the past or present are certain to miss the future."
— John F. Kennedy

Bible Verses:

"Think about the things of heaven, not the things of earth."
-Colossians 3:2 (NLT)

"The beginning of wisdom is this: Get wisdom. Though it cost all you have, get understanding."
-Proverbs 4:7 (NLT)

"If any of you lacks wisdom, you should ask God, who gives generously to all without finding fault, and it will be given to you."
-James 1:5 (NLT)

"For now we see only a reflection as in a mirror; then we shall see face to face. Now I know in part; then I shall know fully, even as I am fully known."
-1 Corinthians 13:12 (NLT)

"For the Lord gives wisdom; from his mouth come knowledge and understanding."
-Proverbs 2:6 (NLT)

"Your word is a lamp for my feet, a light on my path."
-Psalm 119:105 (NLT)

"For the word of God is alive and active. Sharper than any double-edged sword, it penetrates even to dividing soul and spirit, joints and marrow; it judges the thoughts and attitudes of the heart."
-Hebrews 4:12 (NLT)

"There is a time for everything, and a season for every activity under the heavens."
-Ecclesiastes 3:1 (NLT)

"The grass withers and the flowers fall, but the word of our God endures forever."
-Isaiah 40:8 (NLT)

"Do not conform to the pattern of this world, but be transformed by the renewing of your mind. Then you will be able to test and approve what God's will is—his good, pleasing and perfect will."
-Romans 12:2 (NLT)

Today's Affirmations:

- I seek wisdom diligently, knowing it is more valuable than any earthly treasure.
- As I read and study, I am growing in understanding and aligning myself with God's truth.
- I prioritize the Word of God as my guide, trusting that it will light my path in every situation.
- I am open to the new lessons that God reveals through His Word, knowing that each time I read, He speaks to me in fresh ways.
- I trust that my understanding deepens over time, and I embrace the journey of growing closer to God.
- I see my life and circumstances through the lens of God's wisdom, and I trust that He is shaping me for His greater purpose.
- I believe that God's Word is alive and active, speaking to me in every season of my life.
- As I meditate on Scripture, I discover new insights that guide me in every decision and direction.
- I allow God's Word to transform my thoughts and attitudes, knowing that His truth brings clarity and peace.
- I trust that God's timing is perfect and that every season in my life serves a purpose for my growth.
- Though circumstances change, I stand firm in the eternal truth of God's Word, which endures forever.
- I embrace life's transitions with faith, knowing that God is with me, guiding me and revealing new lessons in every season.

with love,
Dad

GRAND RISING DAY TWENTY-FIVE

*One of The Most Important Decisions You Can Make:
The Importance of Choosing The Right Spouse*

One of the most important decisions you'll ever make in life is who you choose as a spouse. Your spouse is not just someone you share a home with; they are your partner in every area of life—your best friend, your business partner, your confidante, your lover. The person you choose can either build you up or break you down.

Research shows that married couples tend to make 70% more income than their single counterparts. Not only that, but married couples tend to live longer and enjoy better health. These statistics reflect a profound truth: marriage is about much more than love. It's about choosing someone who will journey with you through every high and low, helping you become the best version of yourself. In many ways, your spouse is your most important teammate, and together you can either thrive or struggle.

Become the Person You Want to Attract

Before you decide what kind of person you want to marry, it's important to reflect on the qualities you desire in a partner. Do you want someone who is financially responsible? Someone with business acumen or someone who takes care of themselves physically and spiritually? Whatever traits you're looking for, you must first become that person yourself. Like attracts like. If you want a spouse who is disciplined, kind, or successful, you need to develop those qualities in your own life first.

As the African proverb says, "Teeth that are together help each other chew food." Just as teeth work together to break down food, a strong marriage is built when two people with aligned values and goals work together to navigate life. To attract the right person, you must cultivate the same qualities you seek. Only when you are "together together" can you truly form a partnership that thrives.

What the Bible Says About Marriage

The Bible speaks extensively about the importance and sacredness of marriage. Proverbs 18:22 tells us, *"The man who finds a wife finds a treasure, and he receives favor from the Lord."* When you find the right spouse, you are receiving a gift from God. The relationship is not just about companionship but about receiving God's favor through the union.

In Proverbs 31:10, we read, *"Who can find a virtuous and capable wife? She is more precious than rubies."* This verse reminds us that finding a partner with integrity, virtue, and strength is of the highest value—more valuable than wealth or material possessions.

Marriage is a sacred union, as emphasized in Ephesians 5:31 and Matthew 19:5-6: *"A man leaves his father and mother and is joined to his wife, and the two are united into one."* When two people come together in marriage, they are no longer two individuals—they become one. This union is meant to be unbreakable. Jesus himself said, *"Let no one split apart what God has joined together."* (Mark 10:9).

Preparing for a Strong Marriage

So how do you prepare yourself for this sacred union? It starts with being intentional. Make a list of what you want in your future spouse, but also make sure you're working on becoming that person too. If you want someone who is strong in their faith, develop your own spiritual life. If you want someone who is financially responsible, begin to handle your own finances wisely. You can't expect to attract the right person if you're not also putting in the effort to become the right person yourself.

Remember, marriage is a partnership. It's a journey of two people coming together to support one another, build each other up, and face life's challenges as a team. The key is to make sure that when you come together, you are both "together together"—aligned in purpose, vision, and values.

Conclusion: A Union of Purpose

Marriage is more than just finding someone to live with; it's about choosing someone who will help you fulfill God's purpose for your life. It is a partnership where two people become one, supporting each other through every season of life. When you take the time to cultivate the qualities you want in a spouse and trust God to bring the right person into your life, your marriage can be a source of incredible strength and blessing.

As Genesis 2:23 beautifully illustrates, *"This one is bone from my bone, and flesh from my flesh."* Marriage is a bond that runs deeper than emotion—it's a divine connection that unites two people in purpose, faith, and love. Make sure that when you find your spouse, you are ready to be the partner that they need, just as they will be the partner you need.

In our relationships, particularly in marriage, the Bible urges us to be equally yoked. In 2 Corinthians 6:14 (NLT), it says, *"Don't team up with those who are unbelievers. How can righteousness be a partner with wickedness? How can light live with darkness?"* This verse teaches us the importance of spiritual alignment with those we share our lives with.

Being equally yoked means more than just having similar interests or goals—it's about sharing a deep, foundational connection in faith. When two people are yoked together in the same faith, they walk in unity, supporting and uplifting each other through life's challenges. A shared belief in God brings harmony, allowing both partners to grow spiritually together and pursue God's purpose for their lives.

If one person walks in the light and the other in darkness, it creates tension and struggle. Being spiritually misaligned can lead to division, misunderstandings, and a lack of spiritual growth. But when you are equally yoked, you walk together in step with God's plan, nurturing each other and building a stronger relationship rooted in faith.

Ask yourself: Are you walking in step with those around you, especially in your closest relationships? Seek God's guidance in building connections that are aligned with His will, ensuring that you and your partner walk in harmony, yoked together in His love.

Quotes:

"Teeth that are together help each other chew food."

— African Proverb

"A great marriage is not when the 'perfect couple' comes together. It is when an imperfect couple learns to enjoy their differences."

— Dave Meurer

"The secret of a happy marriage is finding the right person. You know they're right if you love to be with them all the time."

— Julia Child

"Marriage is not a noun; it's a verb. It isn't something you get. It's something you do. It's the way you love your partner every day."

— Barbara De Angelis

"We attract hearts by the qualities we display; we retain them by the qualities we possess."

— Jean-Baptiste Antoine Suard

"The best way to find yourself is to lose yourself in the service of others."

— Mahatma Gandhi

"Be the person you want to meet."

— Unknown

"A successful marriage requires falling in love many times, always with the same person."

— Mignon McLaughlin

"Marriage is a partnership, not a dictatorship."

— Unknown

"Coming together is a beginning; keeping together is progress; working together is success."

— Henry Ford

"In the arithmetic of love, one plus one equals everything, and two minus one equals nothing."

— Mignon McLaughlin

Bible Verses:

"Don't team up with those who are unbelievers. How can righteousness be a partner with wickedness? How can light live with darkness?"

-2 Corinthians 6:14 (NLT)

"The man who finds a wife finds a treasure, and he receives favor from the Lord."
Proverbs 18:22 (NLT)

"Who can find a virtuous and capable wife? She is more precious than rubies."
-Proverbs 31:10 (NLT)

"As the Scriptures say, 'A man leaves his father and mother and is joined to his wife, and the two are united into one.'"
-Ephesians 5:31 (NLT)

"And he said, 'This explains why a man leaves his father and mother and is joined to his wife, and the two are united into one.' Since they are no longer two but one, let no one split apart what God has joined together."
-Matthew 19:5-6 (NLT)

"So the Lord God caused the man to fall into a deep sleep. While the man slept, the Lord God took out one of the man's ribs and closed up the opening. Then the Lord God made a woman from the rib, and he brought her to the man. "At last!" the man exclaimed. "This one is bone from my bone, and flesh from my flesh! She will be called 'woman,' because she was taken from 'man.'"
-Genesis 2:21-23 (NLT)

"But 'God made them male and female' from the beginning of creation. This explains why a man leaves his father and mother and is joined to his wife, and the two are united into one.' Since they are no longer two but one, let no one split apart what God has joined together."
-Mark 10:6-9 (NLT)

Today's Affirmations:

- I am intentional in choosing my life partner, knowing that they will be my teammate and support in all things.
- I attract a spouse who aligns with my values, dreams, and purpose, creating a harmonious partnership.
- I recognize the sacredness of marriage and commit to nurturing my relationship with love and respect.
- I embrace the journey of personal growth, becoming the person I want to attract in my future spouse.
- I cultivate qualities such as kindness, responsibility, and strength, knowing that these will attract a like-minded partner.
- I am constantly evolving into a better version of myself, preparing for a loving and supportive partnership."

- I believe that my marriage is a partnership built on love, trust, and mutual respect.
- Together with my spouse, we will overcome challenges and celebrate successes, strengthening our bond.
- I am committed to fostering open communication and teamwork in my relationship, ensuring we are 'together together.
- I cherish the love I share with my spouse and recognize that we are a treasure to one another.
- I trust that God has a purpose for my marriage, and I commit to honoring that purpose every day.
- I celebrate the unity and strength that comes from our relationship, knowing that together we can achieve great things."
- I understand that a strong marriage enriches my life and enhances my well-being.
- I am grateful for the journey of love and partnership, which brings joy and fulfillment to my life.
- I commit to building a marriage that reflects the love and grace of God, creating a legacy of faith and hope.

with love,
Dad

GRAND RISING DAY TWENTY-SIX

GUARD YOUR MIND: PROTECT YOUR THOUGHTS AND PURITY

Our minds are like doorways, constantly open to the influences around us. What we see, hear, and experience enters in, shaping how we think and behave. This is why it's critical to act as vigilant gatekeepers—guarding our minds from harmful influences that lead us away from purity and righteousness.

An experience that shaped my understanding of guarding the mind involves my mentor, Toby. A successful businessman, family man, and spiritual leader, Toby once shared a story about his father, Gary. While attending a sports event, some men nearby were cursing loudly. Gary, though smaller than these men, approached them and sternly asked them to stop, saying his son and other kids were around. His boldness left a lasting impression on Toby, and on me as well.

A similar situation occurred while I was writing this book. I was playing pickleball when a group of young men nearby started cursing during a basketball game. My son and other young kids were within earshot, so I walked over and said, "Hey! Can you watch your language? There are kids nearby." One of the men apologized, and every time my son came close, they quieted down. Toby's story replayed in my mind as I realized that I needed to be the one protecting my son's mind, as well as my own.

This experience reminded me of Philippians 4:8 (NLT):
"Fix your thoughts on what is true, and honorable, and right, and pure, and lovely, and admirable. Think about things that are excellent and worthy of praise."

In today's world, so much is vying for our attention, much of it not beneficial to our spiritual health. Social media, news, entertainment—all of these can feed our minds with negativity or falsehoods if we aren't careful. As we protect our homes from harmful intruders, we must also guard our minds from negative influences. Allowing bitterness, anger, or immorality to take root corrupts our thoughts and actions. In a world filled with distractions, we must be intentional about what we let in through our eye-gate and ear-gate.

That's why guarding our eye-gate and ear-gate is essential. What we let into our minds has the power to grow, for better or worse. We must be mindful of how these influences shape us and, in turn, how we influence others, especially our children.

Protecting your mind doesn't mean shutting out the world, but it does mean making conscious decisions about what you allow to influence you. Be careful of the content you consume, the conversations you engage in, and the thoughts you dwell on. By doing so, you safeguard your purity, your peace, and your walk with God.

Quotes:

"He who controls his own thoughts controls his destiny,"

— Napoleon Hill

"Put a bouncer at the door of your mind!"

— Matt Grotewold

What you focus on expands, and when you focus on the goodness in your life, you create more of."

— Oprah Winfrey

"Be careful what you set your eyes upon. Where you look, you will go."

— Anonymous

"Your mind is a powerful thing. When you fill it with positive thoughts, your life will start to change."

— Anonymous

"Change your thoughts and you change your world."

— Norman Vincent Peale

"Where your mind goes, your energy flows."

— Anonymous

Bible Verses:

"I will refuse to look at anything vile and vulgar. I hate all who deal crookedly; I will have nothing to do with them."
-Psalm 101:3 (NLT)

"Your eye is like a lamp that provides light for your body. When your eye is healthy, your whole body is filled with light. But when your eye is unhealthy, your whole body is filled with darkness. And if the light you think you have is actually darkness, how deep that darkness is!"
-Matthew 6:22-23 (NLT)

"I made a covenant with my eyes not to look with lust at a young woman."
-Job 31:1 (NLT)

"My child, pay attention to what I say. Listen carefully to my words. Don't lose sight of them. Let them penetrate deep into your heart."
-Proverbs 4:20-21 (NLT)

"So faith comes from hearing, that is, hearing the Good News about Christ."
-Romans 10:17 (NLT)

"Tune your ears to wisdom, and concentrate on understanding."
-Proverbs 2:2 (NLT)

"And now, dear brothers and sisters, one final thing. Fix your thoughts on what is true, and honorable, and right, and pure, and lovely, and admirable. Think about things that are excellent and worthy of praise."
-Philippians 4:8 (NLT)

"Don't copy the behavior and customs of this world, but let God transform you into a new person by changing the way you think. Then you will learn to know God's will for you, which is good and pleasing and perfect."
-Romans 12:2 (NLT)

"We destroy every proud obstacle that keeps people from knowing God. We capture their rebellious thoughts and teach them to obey Christ."
-2 Corinthians 10:5 (NLT)

"Think about the things of heaven, not the things of earth."
-Colossians 3:2 (NLT)

Today's Affirmations:

- I choose to keep my eyes away from anything vile or corrupt, focusing only on what is good and pure.
- I will guard my eyes, knowing they are the lamp of my body, and I will fill my life with light by focusing on what is healthy and godly.
- I make a covenant with my eyes to avoid anything that tempts me away from God's path.
- I pay careful attention to wise and godly words, letting them shape my heart and mind.
- I choose to listen to the Good News, allowing it to build and strengthen my faith.
- I am tuning my ears to wisdom and focusing on understanding the truth.
- I fix my thoughts on what is true, honorable, right, pure, lovely, and admirable. I think about things that are excellent and worthy of praise.
- I am transformed by the renewing of my mind, and I focus on God's good, pleasing, and perfect will.
- I take every thought captive and make it obedient to Christ, removing anything that stands against the knowledge of God.
- I set my mind on things above, focusing on heavenly things rather than earthly distractions.

with love,
Dad

GRAND RISING DAY TWENTY-SEVEN

GUARD YOUR HEALTH AND PURITY
(YOUR BODY IS A TEMPLE OF GOD)

In college, I worked out twice a day and was in great shape. It wasn't hard to do back then. I had the time and incentive to stay active. But after graduation, life caught up with me. I got married, became consumed with work, and before long, I let my health slip. I told myself that I was "too busy" to work out, but deep down, I knew I was making excuses. Over time, my health declined, and so did my confidence. I went from being in peak condition to being on six different medications. It was a wake-up call.

What made it worse was the knowledge that I had been raised on a strong foundation of health and wellness. My parents, originally from Jamaica, instilled in me the importance of eating well, using natural remedies, and taking care of the body. Yet here I was, neglecting all of that wisdom. That's when I realized that no amount of success is worth it if you're not healthy enough to enjoy it. I wanted to be in good health not just for myself, but for my children and my family.

Taking care of our bodies goes beyond physical fitness; it involves maintaining purity as well. In a world where sexual immorality is rampant, the message of abstinence may seem outdated, but I believe it's worth talking about. If you're unmarried, I encourage you to abstain from sexual activity and to keep yourself pure. If you've already gone down that path, it's not too late to stop and make a commitment to purity moving forward.

Why is this so important? Your body is a temple of the Holy Spirit. 1 Corinthians 6:19-20 (NLT) says, "Don't you realize that your body is the temple of the Holy Spirit, who lives in you and was given to you by God? You do not belong to yourself, for God bought you with a high price. So you must honor God with your body." When we honor our bodies—by keeping them healthy and pure—we honor God. Whether it's avoiding sexual immorality or taking care of our physical health, these actions reflect the value we place on the gift God has given us.

"Make choices that align with the life God calls you to live."

Abstinence isn't just a spiritual principle; it also carries practical benefits. It helps prevent sexually transmitted infections and unplanned pregnancies, and it avoids the emotional baggage that comes with premature sexual relationships. You'll have more time to focus on your personal goals, friendships, and education, building a solid foundation for your future. Here are some reasons to consider waiting[9]:

- Certainty: A relationship that lasts without sex has a stronger foundation.
- Confidence: You'll know the other person values you for who you are, not for what you can give physically.
- Freedom from worry: There's no fear of unintended pregnancies or STIs.
- Less stress: Waiting allows you time to learn more about yourself and your feelings.
- Self-respect: You'll feel empowered, knowing you stood firm in your values.

As you focus on purity, don't forget about your overall health—mental, emotional, and physical. It's your responsibility to care for your body as a temple of God. This doesn't mean you need to adopt a specific diet or workout regimen, but it does mean paying attention to what your body needs. Eat clean, exercise, and manage stress. Make time for regular checkups and take care of your mental health. These habits not only improve the quality of your life but also honor the Lord who created you.

Good health and purity go hand-in-hand. Guard your heart, mind, and body. Make choices that align with the life God calls you to live. When you take care of your body and your purity, you're not just preserving your physical and emotional well-being—you're honoring the temple that God has entrusted to you.

Quotes:

"Take care of your body. It's the only place you have to live."

— Jim Rohn

"To keep the body in good health is a duty, otherwise we shall not be able to keep our mind strong and clear."

— Buddha

"Health is the greatest gift, contentment the greatest wealth, faithfulness the best relationship."

— Buddha

"The greatest wealth is health."

— Virgil

"Discipline is the bridge between goals and accomplishment."

— Jim Rohn

"The first and greatest victory is to conquer yourself."

— Plato

"Self-discipline begins with the mastery of your thoughts. If you don't control what you think, you can't control what you do."

— Napoleon Hill

"Rule your mind or it will rule you."

— Horace

"The reward of self-discipline is self-respect."

— Anonymous

"True love waits."

— Joshua Harris

"Purity isn't an abstinence from pleasure; it's a commitment to peace."

— Anonymous

"It is health that is real wealth and not pieces of gold and silver."

— Mahatma Gandhi

"You can't enjoy wealth if you're not in good health."

— Anonymous

"Success is not the key to happiness. Happiness is the key to success. If you love what you are doing, you will be successful."

— Albert Schweitzer

Bible Verses:

"Don't let anyone think less of you because you are young. Be an example to all believers in what you say, in the way you live, in your love, your faith, and your purity."
-1 Timothy 4:12 (NLT)

"Make sure that no one is immoral or godless like Esau, who traded his birthright as the firstborn son for a single meal. You know that afterward, when he wanted his father's blessing, he was rejected. It was too late for repentance, even though he begged with bitter tears."
-Hebrews 12:16-17 (NLT)

"Run from sexual sin! No other sin so clearly affects the body as this one does. For sexual immorality is a sin against your own body."
-1 Corinthians 6:18 (NLT)

"Don't you realize that your body is the temple of the Holy Spirit, who lives in you and was given to you by God? You do not belong to yourself, for God bought you with a high price. So you must honor God with your body."
-1 Corinthians 6:19-20 (NLT)

"Don't be impressed with your own wisdom. Instead, fear the Lord and turn away from evil. Then you will have healing for your body and strength for your bones."
-Proverbs 3:7-8 (NLT)

"Because we belong to the day, we must live decent lives for all to see. Don't participate in the darkness of wild parties and drunkenness, or in sexual promiscuity and immoral living, or in quarreling and jealousy. Instead, clothe yourself with the presence of the Lord Jesus Christ. And don't let yourself think about ways to indulge your evil desires."
-Romans 13:13-14 (NLT)

"So put to death the sinful, earthly things lurking within you. Have nothing to do with sexual immorality, impurity, lust, and evil desires. Don't be greedy, for a greedy person is an idolater, worshiping the things of this world."
-Colossians 3:5 (NLT)

"Let there be no sexual immorality, impurity, or greed among you. Such sins have no place among God's people. Obscene stories, foolish talk, and coarse jokes—these are not for you. Instead, let there be thankfulness to God. You can be sure that no immoral, impure, or greedy person will inherit the Kingdom of Christ and of God. For a greedy person is an idolater, worshiping the things of this world. Don't be fooled by those who try to excuse these sins, for the anger of God will fall on all who disobey him. Don't participate in the things these people do. For once you were full of darkness, but now you have light from the Lord. So live as people of light! For this light within you produces only what is good and

right and true."
-Ephesians 5:3-9 (NLT)

Today's Affirmations:

- My body is a temple of the Holy Spirit, and I choose to honor it with care, purity, and discipline.
- I am strong and capable of maintaining a healthy lifestyle that honors God and nurtures my well-being.
- Every day, I choose to make decisions that support my health, mind, and spirit, trusting God's guidance.
- I abstain from sexual immorality, knowing that my worth is rooted in God, not in fleeting physical desires.
- I honor my body by nourishing it with healthy food, regular exercise, and by making choices that promote long-term well-being.
- By choosing purity, I safeguard my emotional and physical health and strengthen my relationship with God.
- I seek wisdom from God to care for my health and maintain balance in all areas of my life.
- I am patient with myself as I rebuild my health, trusting that God will give me strength and guidance.
- I respect myself and others by waiting for the right time and person to express love in a pure and godly way.

with love,
Dad

GRAND RISING
DAY TWENTY-EIGHT

Money Tips

Money is a tool. How we use it not only affects our financial well-being but also reveals our character. Scripture offers timeless wisdom about managing money, and applying these principles will help you honor God and secure your financial future.

Tithe Your Money

One of the first principles of financial stewardship is giving back to God. The tithe, which is giving 10% of your income, honors God with your first fruits. This practice acknowledges that everything we have comes from Him, and it keeps our hearts focused on trusting God for provision rather than trusting solely in money.

Be Generous

Generosity is a reflection of God's character. Giving generously to others not only blesses them but also brings blessings into your own life. Jesus said, *"It is more blessed to give than to receive"* (Acts 20:35). Whether it's your time, money, or talents, live with an open hand, ready to help others.

Pay Yourself First

This principle means prioritizing saving. Before you spend on non-essentials, set aside money for yourself—your future. By paying yourself first, you create a buffer for unexpected expenses and ensure you're building a solid financial foundation. Proverbs 21:20 reminds us, "The wise store up choice food and olive oil, but fools gulp theirs down." Wise people save for tomorrow, while fools spend everything they have today.

Create an Emergency Fund

An emergency fund acts as a financial safety net. Set aside 3-6 months of living expenses to protect yourself from unexpected circumstances like job loss or medical emergencies. It's a sign of wisdom and preparedness, showing that you're not just thinking about the present but also planning for the future.

Stay Out of Debt

Debt is a heavy burden. Romans 13:8 says, *"Owe no one anything except to love one another."* Avoid unnecessary debt and work diligently to pay off what you owe. Debt can hinder your ability to give, save, and live freely. The Bible repeatedly warns about the dangers of being financially enslaved to debt. Paying off debts brings freedom and peace.

Diversify Your Income

Ecclesiastes 11:2 says, *"Divide your investments among many places, for you do not know what risks might lie ahead."* Relying on a single income stream is risky. By diversifying your income, whether through multiple businesses, investments, or side ventures, you create stability and reduce the impact of financial downturns. Just like a farmer who waits for perfect weather never plants, there will never be a perfect time—so start diversifying today.

Mortgage Means "Death Grip"

The word "mortgage" literally translates to "death grip." Be cautious when taking on large amounts of debt, such as mortgages. While owning a home can be a wise investment, you must ensure it's within your means and won't put you in a financial bind. Paying off your mortgage early can relieve a lot of financial stress in the long run.

Save Your Money

Just as you tithe and give to others, remember to save. Whether it's for retirement, future expenses, or an emergency fund, saving is crucial. Proverbs 21:20 teaches us that wise people save, while fools spend everything. Living within your means, saving diligently, and avoiding reckless spending are essential to maintaining financial health.

Managing money with wisdom allows you to live with less stress, more freedom, and greater purpose. By following these biblical principles, you not only secure your financial future but also ensure that your finances align with God's will.

Quotes:

"Do not save what is left after spending, but spend what is left after saving."
— Warren Buffett

"No one has ever become poor by giving."
— Anne Frank

"The meaning of life is to find your gift. The purpose of life is to give it away."
— Pablo Picasso

"A penny saved is a penny earned."
— Benjamin Franklin

"The only sure thing about luck is that it will change."
— Bret Harte

"Too many people spend money they haven't earned, to buy things they don't want, to impress people they don't like."
— Will Rogers

"Debt is the worst poverty."
— Thomas Fuller

"Don't put all your eggs in one basket."
— Traditional Proverb

"The best way to predict the future is to create it."
— Peter Drucker

"The borrower is slave to the lender."
— Dave Ramsey

Bible Verses:

"The generous will prosper; those who refresh others will themselves be refreshed."
-Proverbs 11:25 (NLT)

"You must each decide in your heart how much to give. And don't give reluctantly or in response to pressure. For God loves a person who gives cheerfully.'"
-2 Corinthians 9:7 (NLT)

"Good planning and hard work lead to prosperity, but hasty shortcuts lead to poverty."
-Proverbs 21:5 (NLT)

"Take a lesson from the ants, you lazybones. Learn from their ways and become wise! Though they have no prince or governor or ruler to make them work, they labor hard all summer, gathering food for the winter."
-Proverbs 6:6-8 (NLT)

"A prudent person foresees danger and takes precautions. The simpleton goes blindly on and suffers the consequences."
-Proverbs 22:3 (NLT)

"But divide your investments among many places, for you do not know what risks might lie ahead."
-Ecclesiastes 11:2 (NLT)

"Owe nothing to anyone—except for your obligation to love one another. If you love your neighbor, you will fulfill the requirements of God's law."
-Romans 13:8 (NLT)

"Just as the rich rule the poor, so the borrower is servant to the lender."
-Proverbs 22:7 (NLT)

"Farmers who wait for perfect weather never plant. If they watch every cloud, they never harvest."
-Ecclesiastes 11:4 (NLT)

"Before he left, he called together ten of his servants and divided among them ten pounds, saying, 'Invest this for me while I am gone.'"
-Luke 19:13 (NLT)

"Don't agree to guarantee another person's debt or put up security for someone else. If you can't pay it, even your bed will be snatched from under you."
-Proverbs 22:26-27 (NLT)

"If you are faithful in little things, you will be faithful in large ones. But if you are dishonest in little things, you won't be honest with greater responsibilities."
-Luke 16:10 (NLT)

Today's Affirmations:

- I am generous with my blessings, knowing that giving brings abundance into my life.
- I give cheerfully and with a heart full of gratitude, trusting that God will meet all my needs.
- I prioritize saving and wisely manage my resources for long-term security and prosperity.
- Through discipline and planning, I am building a strong financial foundation.
- I prepare for the future with wisdom, ensuring that I am ready for whatever may come.
- I plan carefully and trust God to guide me in my financial decisions, knowing He provides.
- I live free from the burden of debt, choosing to walk in financial freedom and wisdom.
- I owe nothing but love, and I am wise in my decisions, avoiding unnecessary debt.
- I embrace opportunities to grow and diversify my income streams, ensuring stability for myself and my family.
- I take action and invest my talents wisely, knowing that perfect conditions are not required for progress.
- I manage my finances carefully and avoid unnecessary risks, safeguarding my future and well-being.
- I make wise financial commitments that honor God and protect my family.
- I am faithful with what I have, trusting that small steps of stewardship lead to greater blessings.
- I handle my finances with integrity, knowing that honesty brings success and favor.

with love,
Dad

GRAND RISING DAY TWENTY-NINE

SELF-DEVELOPMENT AND LOVING YOURSELF

There is a fundamental difference between who you are and what you are. What you are represents how you present yourself to the world—the things you do, the roles you fulfill. But who you are is something deeper. It's your core, the inner person, defined by your feelings, attitudes, and values. Developing who you are is essential for living a fulfilling and purpose-driven life.

Self-development is one of the most important things you can do. How can you expect to help others or lead them toward growth if you aren't growing yourself? There's a well-known saying used in airplane safety: "Put on your own oxygen mask first before assisting others." This emphasizes that you must take care of yourself first to be in a position to help others effectively. Likewise, another metaphor says, "You need to be on solid ground before you can throw a life vest to someone else." This shows that ensuring your own stability and security is the foundation for serving others.

You can't give what you don't have. If you don't have your "oxygen mask" or your "life vest," how can you expect to survive, let alone help others?

When my parents passed away in 2015, I found myself in a situation where many family members were leaning on me for strength. I never anticipated this role, and it was overwhelming. But thankfully, by that time, I had spent years developing my mind and spirit. Through mentorship, life coaching, reading, listening to audiobooks, and following podcasts on leadership and self-development, I built a strong foundation that helped me navigate one of the toughest moments of my life Without that preparation, I wouldn't have had the emotional and mental resources to support others in their grief.

If you want to lead others, you must first learn to lead yourself. Self-discipline, emotional maturity, and personal growth are prerequisites for effective leadership. As Jim Rohn said, "Formal education will make you a living; self-education will make you a fortune." This isn't just about financial wealth but the wealth of wisdom, strength, and resilience you can develop through intentional self-growth.

Aristotle reminds us that "We are what we repeatedly do. Excellence, then, is not an act, but a habit." Personal growth and excellence aren't defined by one-time achievements; they are a result of the daily habits and decisions that shape our lives over time.

There's a journey that every person must take, and it's not across countries or through careers—it's within. George Bernard Shaw said it best: "Life isn't about finding yourself; it's about creating yourself." Every day, you have the opportunity to craft and refine who you are, shedding what no longer serves you and adding the qualities that align with your true self.

Confucius also reminds us, "They must often change, who would be constant in happiness or wisdom." Personal growth requires change, adaptation, and a willingness to be uncomfortable as you push past your limits.

Loving yourself isn't about vanity or selfishness. It's about recognizing your worth as God's creation and honoring that by investing in your well-being—mentally, physically, and spiritually. As Oscar Wilde once said, "To love oneself is the beginning of a lifelong romance." It's a relationship that sets the tone for every other relationship in your life. When you nurture a healthy, loving relationship with yourself, you become better equipped to love others well.

Quotes:

"Make Personal Growth a daily priority"
— John Maxwell

"You have power over your mind—not outside events. Realize this, and you will find strength."
— Marcus Aurelius

"What lies behind us and what lies before us are tiny matters compared to what lies within us."
— Ralph Waldo Emerson

"The only journey is the one within."
— Rainer Maria Rilke

"We cannot direct the wind, but we can adjust the sails."
— Dolly Parton

"Do not wait for leaders; do it alone, person to person."
— Mother Teresa

"Knowing yourself is the beginning of all wisdom."
— Aristotle

"Success is to be measured not so much by the position that one has reached in life as by the obstacles which he has overcome."
— Booker T. Washington

"It's not about finding yourself, it's about creating yourself."
— George Bernard Shaw

"Your task is not to seek for love, but merely to seek and find all the barriers within yourself that you have built against it."
— Rumi

"The best way to find yourself is to lose yourself in the service of others."
— Mahatma Gandhi

"He who conquers others is strong; He who conquers himself is mighty."
— Lao Tzu

"Formal education will make you a living; self-education will make you a fortune."
— Jim Rohn

Bible Verses:

"But the Holy Spirit produces this kind of fruit in our lives: love, joy, peace, patience, kindness, goodness, faithfulness, gentleness, and self-control. There is no law against these things!"

-Galatians 5:22-23 (NLT)

"Search me, O God, and know my heart; test me and know my anxious thoughts."

-Psalm 139:23 (NLT)

"This means that anyone who belongs to Christ has become a new person. The old life is gone; a new life has begun!"

-2 Corinthians 5:17 (NLT)

"For I can do everything through Christ, who gives me strength."

-Philippians 4:13 (NLT)

"A second is equally important: 'Love your neighbor as yourself.'"

-Matthew 22:39 (NLT)

"For the Lord grants wisdom! From his mouth come knowledge and understanding."

-Proverbs 2:6) (NLT)

"Anyone who listens to my teaching and follows it is wise, like a person who builds a house on solid rock."

-Matthew 7:24 (NLT)

"Don't copy the behavior and customs of this world, but let God transform you into a new person by changing the way you think."

-Romans 12:2 (NLT)

"Dear brothers and sisters, when troubles of any kind come your way, consider it an opportunity for great joy. For you know that when your faith is tested, your endurance has a chance to grow."

-James 1:2-3 (NLT)

"'For I know the plans I have for you,' says the Lord. 'They are plans for good and not for disaster, to give you a future and a hope.'"

-Jeremiah 29:11 (NLT)

Today's Affirmations:

- I embrace my true self, knowing that I am more than my external circumstances.
- I am committed to my personal growth and recognize the strength that comes from within.
- I am a new creation in Christ; I let go of the past and embrace my new

life with joy.
- I love myself deeply and recognize that self-love empowers me to love others well.
- I actively seek wisdom and understanding, knowing that they lead to personal growth.
- I build my life on a solid foundation, making wise choices that reflect my values.
- I welcome change and transformation, allowing God to renew my mind and spirit.
- I view challenges as opportunities for growth and embrace each trial with joy.
- I trust in God's plans for my life, knowing they are filled with hope and a bright future.
- I am capable of achieving my goals, and I take action each day toward my dreams.
- I absorb what is useful, release what no longer serves me, and create the best version of myself.
- I am continually growing and evolving, dedicated to becoming my best self.
- I have the power to create my own path and shape my destiny through self-awareness.
- I honor my journey of self-discovery and am grateful for the progress I have made.

with love,
Dad

GRAND RISING DAY THIRTY

Look For Someone To Help and Be Generous

The Bible frequently emphasizes the power and blessing of generosity, reminding us that giving is an expression of love, faith, and obedience to God. When my wife and I began supporting the West Volusia Dream Center, in Orange City, Florida we were acting in alignment with Scripture's call to serve the needy. By offering food, mentorship, and support to those facing hardship, the Dream Center embodies Proverbs 19:17: *"Whoever is kind to the poor lends to the Lord."* In giving to others, we not only fulfill God's commands but also open ourselves up to His blessings.

In 2019, our pastor Jamie Jones declared it the "Year of Freedom," aiming to pay off our church's debt to sow more into ministries. Inspired by that vision, our church worked together, and soon after, the Dream Center was born. This organization serves families in need, offering food, mentorship, and other essential services. It's amazing how when we pour into others, God blesses both the giver and receiver. As Luke 6:38 reminds us, *"Give, and it will be given to you."*

Generosity extends beyond mere financial contributions; it includes time, compassion, and action. God calls us to be stewards of what He has entrusted to us. Whether we are offering a meal to someone hungry or mentoring a person in need of guidance, we reflect His heart. James 1:27 reminds us that true religion is *"to look after orphans and widows in their distress."* Supporting ministries like the West Volusia Dream Center is one way to live this out.

I've witnessed firsthand the transformation that generosity brings. When our church paid off its debt, we collectively saw how freeing ourselves from financial bondage allowed us to invest more in our community. The Bible says, "Faith without works is dead" (James 2:26), and that was never clearer to us than when our church took action.

When you look to help others you take the focus off of yourself and your own problems. Mother Teresa said, "We cannot do great things. We can only do little things with great love." You will be amazed at the sense of strength, self-worth, and satisfaction you feel when you meet the needs of others. Generosity, whether large or small, creates a ripple effect, impacting both the giver and the receiver. The truth is, when we focus on helping others, our own burdens lighten. We see the world through the lens of love and purpose, which transforms our own hearts in the process.

Luke 6:38 captures this beautifully: *"Give, and it will be given to you: good measure, pressed down, shaken together, and running over."* When we open our hands to help others, God opens His to pour blessings into our lives—blessings not just of wealth, but of joy, peace, and fulfillment. Feel free to check out the great things the Dream Center is doing in the community:

West Volusia Dream Center
www.westvolusiadreamcenter.com

Quotes:

"I believe you can do well (financially) and do good (give back to the community) at the same time."

— Magic Johnson

"No one has ever become poor by giving."

— Anne Frank

"The best way to find yourself is to lose yourself in the service of others."

— Mahatma Gandhi

"We make a living by what we get. We make a life by what we give."

— Winston Churchill

"It is not how much we give, but how much love we put into giving."

— Mother Teresa

GRAND RISING DAY THIRTY

"The meaning of life is to find your gift. The purpose of life is to give it away."

— Pablo Picasso

Bible Verses:

"If you help the poor, you are lending to the Lord—and he will repay you!"
-Proverbs 19:17 (NLT)

"If someone has enough money to live well and sees a brother or sister in need but shows no compassion—how can God's love be in that person?"
-1 John 3:17 (NLT)

"Give, and you will receive. Your gift will return to you in full—pressed down, shaken together to make room for more, running over, and poured into your lap. The amount you give will determine the amount you get back."
-Luke 6:38 (NLT)

"Blessed are those who are generous, because they feed the poor."
-Proverbs 22:9 (NLT)

"Pure and genuine religion in the sight of God the Father means caring for orphans and widows in their distress and refusing to let the world corrupt you."
-James 1:27 (NLT)

"Feed the hungry, and help those in trouble. Then your light will shine out from the darkness, and the darkness around you will be as bright as noon."
-Isaiah 58:10 (NLT)

"Remember this—a farmer who plants only a few seeds will get a small crop. But the one who plants generously will get a generous crop. You must each decide in your heart how much to give. And don't give reluctantly or in response to pressure. For God loves a person who gives cheerfully.'"
-2 Corinthians 9:6-7 (NLT)

"Watch out! Don't do your good deeds publicly, to be admired by others, for you will lose the reward from your Father in heaven. When you give to someone in need, don't do as the hypocrites do—blowing trumpets in the synagogues and streets to call attention to their acts of charity! I tell you the truth, they have received all the reward they will ever get. But when you give to someone in need, don't let your left hand know what your right hand is doing. Give your gifts in private, and your Father, who sees everything, will reward you."
-Matthew 6:1-4 (NLT)

"Cornelius stared at him in terror. 'What is it, sir?' he asked the angel. And the angel replied, 'Your prayers and gifts to the poor have been received by God as an offering!'"
-Acts 10:4 (NLT)

Today's Affirmations:

- I am blessed as I give generously, knowing that God rewards those who help others.
- I reflect God's love by showing compassion to those in need.
- When I give, I open the door for God's abundant blessings to flow back into my life.
- My generosity brings joy, peace, and fulfillment, as I follow God's heart in caring for others.
- Every act of kindness I offer strengthens my faith and helps me grow closer to God.
- I give cheerfully, knowing that God sees my heart and blesses my sincere generosity.
- My light shines brightest when I help those in need, transforming both their lives and mine.
- I focus on giving with love, not for recognition, trusting God to reward my humility.
- I find purpose and meaning in serving others, knowing that even small acts of love make a difference.
- By giving, I experience greater self-worth and joy, aligning my actions with God's will.

with love,
Dad

GRAND RISING DAY THIRTY-ONE

Finish What You Started / Finish Strong

Success is not merely a destination; it's the pursuit of a worthy dream and goal, a journey that requires commitment and perseverance. It's not just about starting; it's about having the courage to finish what you began. As an anonymous quote wisely states, "The cowards never start, the weak never finish, and the strong never quit."

Three Types of People

In life, there are three types of people: Quitters, Campers, and Climbers.[10] Quitters give up at the first sign of difficulty. Campers climb partway up the mountain but settle for less than their potential. Climbers, on the other hand, keep moving forward, refusing to quit until they reach the summit. I aspire to be a Climber, steadfast in my pursuit of God's plans for my life.

The Climb

To achieve what we desire—be it a fulfilling marriage, a successful career, or a deep faith—we must embrace the climb. Life isn't always easy or straightforward; it's often a rocky path filled with challenges and detours. But if we persist in climbing, we will uncover the abundant plans God has in store for us. As Jentezen Franklin reminds us, "If you quit, you'll never see all that God has for you. If you camp, you'll settle for less than God's best. But if you climb, you'll discover His plans for you."

Learning Through Adversity

Bill Belichick once said, "You can't learn how to consistently win until you learn how to not consistently lose." This philosophy highlights the importance of learning from failures and building habits that lead to success. Every setback is an opportunity for growth, teaching us resilience and fortitude.

The Courage to Continue

Success is not final, and failure is not fatal; it is the courage to continue that counts. As Winston S. Churchill stated, "It's not whether you get knocked down, it's whether you get up." Life's journey will undoubtedly have its ups and downs, but each day presents a new opportunity to finish what we've started and to make each moment count.

Remember Ralph Waldo Emerson's words: "Finish each day and be done with it. You have done what you could." Let's strive to be Climbers, embracing the journey with diligence and perseverance, knowing that the road to success is filled with challenges—but also rich with rewards.

Reflection:

- As we pursue our goals, let us hold on to these affirmations:
- I have the strength to finish what I started.
- I will not settle for less than what God has planned for me.
- I embrace the challenges, knowing they shape my character.
- I will keep climbing, trusting that my perseverance will lead to greater rewards.

In this journey of faith and purpose, let us finish strong, knowing that our dedication and hard work will lead us to the fulfillment of our dreams.

Quotes:

"It's not over until it's over"
— Yogi Berra.

"Diligence is the mother of good luck."
— Benjamin Franklin

"Success is not final; failure is not fatal: It is the courage to continue that counts."
— Winston S. Churchill

"It's not whether you get knocked down, it's whether you get up."
— Vince Lombardi

"The only way to finish is to start."
— Anonymous

"You can't finish what you don't start, but you can finish what you start."
— Anonymous

"Great works are performed not by strength but by perseverance."
— Samuel Johnson

"Finish each day and be done with it. You have done what you could."
— Ralph Waldo Emerson

"The road to success is dotted with many tempting parking spaces."
— Will Rogers

"Don't count the days; make the days count."
— Muhammad Ali

"The price of greatness is responsibility."
— Winston S. Churchill

"When you finish your work, you'll know what to do next."
— Anonymous

Bible Verses:

'Jesus looked at them intently and said, 'Humanly speaking, it is impossible. But with God everything is possible.'''
-Matthew 19:26 (NLT)

"Then you will not become spiritually dull and indifferent. Instead, you will follow the example of those who are going to inherit God's promises because of their faith and endurance."
-Hebrews 6:12 (NLT)

"So let's not get tired of doing what is good. At just the right time we will reap a harvest of blessing if we don't give up."
-Galatians 6:9 (NLT)

"And I am certain that God, who began the good work within you, will continue his work until it is finally finished on the day when Christ Jesus returns."
-Philippians 1:6 (NLT):

Today's Affirmations:

- I have the strength and courage to finish everything I start.
- I will not settle for anything less than God's best for my life.
- I embrace challenges as opportunities to grow and develop my character.
- I am committed to climbing higher, trusting that perseverance brings greater rewards.
- Each setback is a lesson, and I will rise stronger every time I fall.
- I will make every day count and strive for success with diligence.
- I believe that with God, all things are possible, and I will keep moving forward.

Let these affirmations guide you as you pursue your goals and finish strong!

Excerpts from the song "Till the Day I Die"
by Toby Mac Featuring NF

"I'll keep swingin' for the fences / It's like this heart is defenseless / Against the passion that's pumpin' through my veins. / Blood, sweat, tears, it's a callin' / And if I can't walk, then I'm crawlin' / It might flicker, but they can't kill the flame."

"I can't stop, I can't quit / It's in my heart, it's on my lips. / I can't stop, no, I can't quit / It's in my heart, yeah, I'm all in / 'Til the wheels fall off / 'Til the spotlight fades / I will lift Your banner high."

"And 'til the walls crash in / For the rest of my days / I'll lay it all on the line / 'Til the day I / 'Til the day I die."

"This ain't religion, it's devotion / 3-6-5, every minute, every day."

"'Til the wheels fall off / 'Til the spotlight fades."

Conclusion

As we reflect on our journeys, may we embody the spirit of Climbers. Let our hearts burn with passion, our resolve remains steadfast, and our faith guide us through every challenge. Together, let us lift our banners high and finish strong, knowing that our commitment and hard work will lead us to a fulfilling life of purpose.

with love,
Dad

GRAND RISING DAY THIRTY-TWO

It's Your Turn!

You've journeyed through these pages and seen the beliefs and values that I hold close—truths I long to pass on to my children, guiding them toward a future anchored in hope, strength, and faith. But this book isn't just about my story or my legacy. Now, I leave this final chapter to you.

Whether you're my son, my daughter, or a fellow traveler in faith, this chapter is yours to write. Take a moment to reflect on the lessons God has written in your own life. What truths will you pass on? What legacy will you leave for those who follow after you?

Think about the challenges you've overcome, the blessings you've received, and the faith that has carried you through it all. Your story matters—every victory, every struggle, every step of faith. As you write your own chapter, may it be a testament to God's grace at work in your life, a beacon of hope for generations to come.

So, what will your chapter say? The pen is in your hands.

Quotes:

Bible Verses:

GRAND RISING DAY THIRTY-TWO

Today's Affirmations:

Go Placidly Amid the Noise and Haste

"Go placidly amid the noise and haste, and remember what peace there may be in silence. As far as possible without surrender be on good terms with all persons. Speak your truth quietly and clearly; and listen to others, even the dull and the ignorant; they too have their story. Avoid loud and aggressive persons, they are vexations to the spirit. If you compare yourself with others, you may become vain and bitter; for always there will be greater and lesser persons than yourself. Enjoy your achievements as well as your plans. Keep interested in your own career, however humble; it is a real possession in the changing fortunes of time. Exercise caution in your business affairs; for the world is full of trickery. But let this not blind you to what virtue there is; many persons strive for high ideals; and everywhere life is full of heroism. Be yourself. Especially, do not feign affection. Neither be cynical about love; for in the face of all aridity and disenchantment it is as perennial as the grass. Take kindly the counsel of the years, gracefully surrendering the things of youth. Nurture strength of spirit to shield you in sudden misfortune. But do not distress yourself with dark imaginings. Many fears are born of fatigue and loneliness. Beyond a wholesome discipline, be gentle with yourself. You are a child of the universe, no less than the trees and the stars; you have a right to be here. And whether or not it is clear to you, no doubt the universe is unfolding as it should. Therefore be at peace with God, whatever you conceive Him to be, and whatever your labors and aspirations, in the noisy confusion of life keep peace with your soul. With all its sham, drudgery, and broken dreams, it is still a beautiful world. Be cheerful."

Strive to be happy.

— Found in Old Saint Paul's Church, Baltimore. Dated 1692[11]

May the good Lord bless you and keep you, guiding you all the days of your life. May His blessings extend to generation after generation, that your family may walk in His favor. AMEN!

> *"Being confident of this very thing, that He who has begun a good work in you will complete it until the day of Jesus Christ."*
> -Philippians 1:6 (NKJV)

Always remember, your Daddy will ALWAYS love you. I prayed for you even before you were born. Your Father in heaven created you for greatness, and you WILL do great things! Stand on my shoulders and see the promised land. You are built for greatness. Now go out and be great! We are so proud of you. Now, it's your turn to write the chapters of your life's book and pass it on to your children's children.

With all my love,

Dad

A CHANGED LIFE CHANGES LIVES;
BE THE ONE!

Please purchase the companion journal that accompanies this book!

The companion journal is designed to help you dive deeper into the lessons shared in Legacy of Wisdom. It provides guided prompts, reflection questions, and space to record your thoughts as you apply these principles to your life. It's more than a journal—it's a tool to help you turn wisdom into action and create your legacy

Also available everywhere books are sold!

BOOK RECOMMENATIONS

Life & Thought Process:

- The Bible - God
- The Left Handed Warrior - Jamie Jones
- Hung by the Tongue - Francis P. Martin
- The Way to Live 1.0 - Joshua Keith Craft
- Master Key to Riches - Napoleon Hill
- Think and Grow Rich - Napoleon Hill
- The Magic of Thinking Big - David J. Schwartz
- What to Say When You Talk to Yourself - Dr. Shad Helmstetter
- The Burden of Freedom - Dr. Miles Monroe
- Outwitting The Devil - Napoleon Hill/Sharon Lechter

People Skills:

- How to Win Friends and Influence People - Dale Carnegie
- Many Communicate Few Connect - Dr. John C. Maxwell
- Bringing out the best in people - Aubrey C. Daniels
- Skill With People - Les Giblin

Focus & Productivity:

- The Compound Effect - Darren Hardy
- The Slight Edge - Jeff Olson
- The Gap & The Gain - Benjamin Hardy
- The Breakthrough Code - Tom McCarthy

Relationship:

- The 5 Love Languages - Gary Chapman
- Love and Respect - Dr. Emerson Eggerichs
- His Needs Her Needs - William T. Harley
- The Love Code - Alexander Loyd PhD, ND

Leadership:

- Becoming a Leader - Dr. Miles Munroe
- Leadership 101 - Dr. John C. Maxwell
- The 21 irrefutable laws of leadership - Dr. John C. Maxwell
- The Self Aware Leader - Dr. John C. Maxwell
- Martin Luther King Jr. On Leadership - Donald T. Phillips

Endnotes

1. Census.gov
https://www.census.gov/library/stories/2021/04/number-of-children-living-only-with-their-mothers-has-doubled-in-past-50-years.html
2. Pew Research Center:
https://www.pewresearch.org/short-reads/2019/12/12/u-s-children-more-likely-than-children-in-other-countries-to-live-with-just-one-parent/
3. www.liveabout.com:
https://www.liveabout.com/fatherless-children-in-america-statistics-1270392
4. The Mamba Mentality: How I Play (2018).
https://medium.com/@RationalBadger/mamba-mentality-cc986cb67cdd
5. Pastor Keith Craft "Choose Your Hard"
6. University of Rochester Medical Center
Medical Reviewers: Callie Tayrien, RN MSN; Stacey Wojcik, MBA BSN RN; Steven Kang MD
7. "The Pursuit" Mentors & Proteges
8. 6 Ways to Develop a Heart and Attitude of Gratitude is an Excerpt from Pastor Jamie Jones (Trinity Church Deltona) Sermon, 9.15.24
9. Reference: https://www.bemidjistate.edu/services/health-education/sexual-health/advantages-of-abstinence/
10. Excerpt from Jentzen Franklin Devotional (Quitters, Campers, and Climbers) 7.29.24 https://jentezenfranklin.org/
11. Go Placidly Amid the Noise and Haste:
-Found in Old Saint Paul's Church, Baltimore. Dated 1692